Effective Interventions and for Pupils with SEND

Effective Interventions and Strategies for Pupils with SEND offers practical, tried-and-tested strategies for supporting and championing pupils with special educational needs and disabilities. Each strategy has been researched, trialled and reviewed, with the results presented accessibly and the concerns of real teachers a key focus of the discussion.

With each chapter written by an experienced and innovative teacher working with children with SEND, this book covers a wide range of strategies for supporting pupils with SEND. These effective strategies include:

- Using a 'daily run' to improve concentration and behaviour
- Creating SEN champions and more effective teaching assistants
- Embedding anxiety-reducing strategies in the classroom.

Written for teachers by teachers, *Effective Interventions and Strategies for Pupils with SEND* is an indispensable resource for all SENCOs and other educators and staff working with children with special educational needs looking to provide the best learning experiences possible.

Gill Richards is Emeritus Professor of Special Education, Equity and Inclusion at Nottingham Trent University, UK.

Jane Starbuck is the Strategic Leader for Inclusion for a large partnership of schools and is the Deputy Regional Leader for East Midlands, South Yorkshire and the Humber for 'Whole School SEND'.

A View into the Classroom

Series edited by Gill Richards

A View into the Classroom is a unique series, written by and for education practitioners. Supported throughout with real-life case studies of success, books in this series offer easy access to practical school-based education research for a wide range of teachers who want to understand more about issues that interest and challenge them. With the current focus on 'evidence-based practice' in education settings, all teachers increasingly need to become 'research literate', so these accounts will provide valuable insight for any teacher about manageable research processes that can be incorporated into their own professional activities to become more effective in the classroom, with greater impact on their students.

Effective Interventions and Strategies for Pupils with SEND
Using Evidence-Based Methods for Maximum Impact
Gill Richards and Jane Starbuck

Reducing Teachers' Marking Workload and Developing Pupils' Learning
How to Create More Impact with Less Marking
Gill Richards and Rhian Richardson

Effective Interventions and Strategies for Pupils with SEND

Using Evidence-Based Methods for Maximum Impact

Edited by
Gill Richards and Jane Starbuck

Routledge
Taylor & Francis Group

LONDON AND NEW YORK

First published
by Routledge
2 Park Square, Milton Park, Abingdon, Oxon OX14 4RN

and by Routledge
52 Vanderbilt Avenue, New York, NY 10017

Routledge is an imprint of the Taylor & Francis Group, an informa business

British Library Cataloguing in Publication Data
A catalogue record for this book is available from the British Library

Library of Congress Cataloging-in-Publication Data
A catalog record has been requested for this book

ISBN: 978-0-367-19796-4 (hbk)
ISBN: 978-0-367-19797-1 (pbk)
ISBN: 978-0-429-24331-8 (ebk)

Typeset in Sabon
by Taylor & Francis Books

Contents

Acknowledgements

We would like to thank all of the teachers, pupils and their schools for contributing towards these projects. We would also like to thank Alison Foyle (Senior Publisher) for her encouragement of this new venture with teachers' research and the team at Routledge for their support in ensuring that our book was ready for publication.

A special thanks to Michele Taylor, our wonderful administrator at Nottingham Trent University, whose skills and unfailing patience made a major contribution to preparing the final stages of this book.

Contributors

Gill Richards is Emeritus Professor of Special Education, Equity and Inclusion at Nottingham Trent University. Prior to this, she taught in mainstream and special schools for 21 years. She has been a project leader for government funded SEN projects in UK schools and a European Erasmus project on behaviour management in Greece with teachers. Her recent research includes a NCTL project on teachers' workload, a project on the impact of teachers' action research in schools, and an eight-year study of the aspirations and achievements of girls living in an area of severe deprivation. She currently teaches on the National Award for SENCOs and supports schools in developing their own research culture.

Jane Starbuck was a SENCO and primary school headteacher. She is currently the Strategic Leader for Inclusion for a large partnership of schools and is the Deputy Regional Leader for East Midlands, South Yorkshire and the Humber for 'Whole School SEND'. Jane has a particular interest in developing a strategic-based approach to SEND provision in schools. She has established effective collaborations between schools in order to develop specialist provision, alternative provision, training and sharing resources. Jane is also a lecturer on the National SENCO Award for Nottingham Trent University.

Clare Bedford has been a primary school teacher since 2009, having trained in Early Childhood Studies through a B.Ed. degree at the University of Plymouth. She became a SENDCO in 2012 and completed her National Award for Special Educational Needs in 2015. She is a trained 'Thrive' practitioner, holding a licence for this since 2013. Clare works as SENDCO across two schools in an Academy in the South of England and has a specialist interest in Social, Emotional and Mental Health. She has been involved in delivering training to Newly Qualified Teachers through a teaching school, supporting them on behaviour management, in addition to running parenting workshops.

Amy Breeze has been a teacher since 2006, working in both secondary and sixth form settings. She currently teaches 'A' Level English and Drama. Amy completed an MA in Performing Arts Education in 2011 at the Liverpool Institute of Performing Arts. In 2015, she completed a PGDip in Special Educational Needs Coordination to become a qualified SENCO, building on the work she began the previous year in improving the monitoring and transition of students with SEN. Amy is an enthusiastic advocate for student welfare; she has trained as Mental Health First Aider and continues to develop her practice in this field.

Rosemary Brooks has been a secondary school teacher since 1982, teaching Modern Languages and English. She has worked in a boys' grammar school since 1995 and has been involved in pastoral leadership since 2003, holding posts as Key Stage 3 Manager and Head of Year 7 and Transition. She became SENCO in 2015, completing the National Award for SEN Co-ordination in 2016. As part of a phased retirement plan she is now working part-time, focusing on her role of SENCO and managing the universal student support service. Most recently, she led the school's successful bid to achieve the Well-Being Award for Schools.

Katherine Chubb has worked as a primary school teacher in a range of schools since completing her teacher training at Homerton College, University of Cambridge, in 2003. In 2014, she was appointed as Special Educational Needs Coordinator within her school and has strived to ensure the school provides an inclusive environment where all children can flourish. Her interest in improving outcomes for all children was an important focus while she was completing the National Award For SEN Coordination. She was appointed as Assistant Headteacher in 2018 at her school, while continuing in her role as SENCO.

Laura Inglis has been a primary school teacher since 2009 and became a Support Teacher for children with special educational needs in 2018. She has experience of working as a SENCO in an infant school and during that time achieved the National Award for SEN Co-ordination. In her current role she provides support for children with funding to be fully included within their school and works alongside schools to develop their practice.

Lara Krause qualified with a PGCE in 2013 and has worked in her current school since she was a NQT. She has taught in Year 2 and Year 3, and currently runs the school's nursery. She took on the SENCO role in 2015 and completed the National Award in SEN Co-ordination in 2016. Her role includes mentoring NQTs and BA teaching students in her school. Lara is currently taking part in a maths research project with her local authority to improve and increase mathematical opportunities within the EYFS.

Maxine Siddall has been a primary school teacher since 1993 after graduating at Liverpool St John Moore's University. She taught for five years in the UK before moving to Switzerland for two years and teaching at an International School in Montreux. Following this, in 2001 she became the Special Needs Coordinator at a school in Yorkshire for four years, which then became her passion. Maxine has been working at a school in the East Midlands since 2005 and is a member of the SLT, SENCO, Designated Teacher for Looked After Children and Leader for trainee students and NQTs. In 2017 she completed part of a Master's Study for the Designated Teacher for Children in Care Award and has since worked closely with a Virtual School on a project to become an Attachment Aware School.

Katherine Smith began teaching as a primary school teacher in 2002 and became a SENCO in 2006. Soon after her qualifying year Katherine began a Postgraduate Diploma in Special Education Needs. In 2016 she completed her National Award for SEN Co-ordination. Katherine is a keen researcher with an interest in education policy; her research on raising the profile of the SENCO was exhibited at the NASEN Live Event in 2017. Also in 2017, Katherine passed her MA in Special and Additional Education Needs, with distinction. Katherine also enjoys her role as the SEND Governor at her daughter's primary school.

Jill Turner has been a primary school teacher since 2000, following several years as a TA in a school for children with profound and multiple learning difficulties. She became a SENCO in 2013 and an SLE (Specialist Leader of Education) for mainstream primary SEN in 2019. Since 2013 she has been working in a school located in an area of high deprivation where she has worked on a variety of strategies to help to improve the outcomes for children with SEN, particularly 'Social, Emotional and Mental Health' and 'Speech, Communication and Language Needs'.

Sorcha Walmsley has been a primary school teacher since 2011. She has taught across different phases and has supported children with a range of SEN, both within her own classroom and as a SENCO. She has worked in inner-city schools in the Midlands and now works as a SENCO in an Enhanced Resource Primary School. She has taught in schools where an 'Evidence-Based Teaching' approach has been at the heart of good provision and through this, she has piloted and implemented change that has helped improve outcomes for children.

Introduction

Jane Starbuck and Gill Richards

A 'Leader of SEND' view

It has been an absolute privilege to be involved with this book and to read the work of these authors. The word 'research' has, until recently, filled many teachers, including myself, with fear – having visions of thousands of questionnaires and complicated statistical analysis. These chapters demonstrate that this is not the case, with each showing that research can be small-scale, practical and relevant to what is happening in our classrooms – an activity that teachers can carry out without a negative impact on their workload.

In reality, we need to be doing more research in schools to ensure the interventions and projects we implement are having the desired impact. Without this, how do we know if our good intentions are making a difference for the most vulnerable pupils? Are we seeing a positive impact where we most want to see it, be this academic or social and emotional?

Schools are increasingly being called upon to identify 'value for money' principles regarding interventions. Small-scale practical research – like the studies in this book – gives SENCOs (Special Educational Needs Co-ordinators) and other teachers the opportunity to reflect on what is working and, equally, what isn't. It can provide quality assurance and evidence of impact to support the value of maintaining interventions, which in these times of financial challenges and pressures on time is vital to demonstrate to Senior Leadership Teams. The SENCOs' research in this book demonstrates the impact of interventions they have introduced and, importantly, also raises the profile of their role in school because they involved wider stakeholders from the school community.

I believe the value of this book is that any teacher will be able to read it on two levels: first, to identify with small-scale research on activities they may be using or introducing in school, so these will act as an evidence base; and second – and more importantly – I hope it inspires others, especially SENCOs, to get involved in evidence-based research of their own. The SENCO is in a pivotal role to be able to carry out research in school. We all have introduced new schemes, practices or interventions and turning them into research projects enables us to measure impact and capture the voices of those involved, especially the young people for whom they are devised.

Much of the evidence that is currently available has not been carried out by people working in schools, so research on this small, practical scale provides us with an evidence base from practitioners who understand the real challenges facing schools when supporting children with SEND. I believe it is this that makes our book both unique and invaluable: it encapsulates the honest views of SENCOs who are working every day with staff and children and highlights current areas of interest and concern.

Jane Starbuck

Teaching and learning: students with Special Educational Needs and Disability (SEND)

I started my early teaching career working in specialist education settings where young people were sent by the UK court system to complete their schooling. I often wondered why some of these young people behaved in the way that they did when this so clearly created troublesome situations for them. A few years later, as a mainstream school teacher, I also wondered why some of my teaching didn't seem to result in a good learning experience for students. When I became an evening part-time youth leader in the same area in which I taught, I realised that we only see part of young people's lives and that many are managing all kinds of experiences that affect their learning. It was these concerns that encouraged me to investigate issues that impacted on 'vulnerable' students and their educational opportunities.

Young people with SEND experience a wide range of interventions and support strategies in schools. Already facing disadvantage in their learning, it is important that these students receive clear benefits from any intervention or strategy provided to them. This means that teachers and SENCOs need to be assured of the quality of claims made about expected impact and, importantly, evaluate their effectiveness with specific student (s) using them in school, so that valuable learning time and resources are not wasted. Research should play a part in decision-making here – first, in the selection of *tested* interventions and strategies, and second in checking that these are working effectively for individual students. Providing evidence of this not only identifies what learning is taking place, but also enables schools to show how they are meeting Ofsted's inspection guidance (2019) that all learners, particularly those with SEND, are receiving a high-grade, ambitious education that meets their needs.

Teachers and 'evidence informed teaching and learning'

There is a growing interest from teachers in education research that relates clearly to 'their world'. Until recently, most research was carried out by professional researchers with focused funding. Teachers often criticised this 'academic' research as being inaccessible – either to obtain or to read – or difficult to apply within their own unique school situation. Understandably, they questioned if academics even saw them as an intended audience for sharing the results of their research.

I recently carried out a small-scale research study (52 participants) to discover what teachers, SENCOs and their headteachers thought about taking part in school-based research – below are a few of their comments which capture some of the benefits and previous misconceptions:

> I thought that research was mostly conducted by 'experts' – those not working in schools. Now I know it is a useful way of getting clear insight into how something is working and we should not assume we always know what is best for pupils. (Teacher)

> I thought it was something that only 'academics' did from an office! Now I realise that research is about real life issues going on in ordinary schools and can be done by staff who work there. (SENCO)

> I had never given it any thought, never seen it in practice or thought it to be useful. Now I realise that it helps focus priorities for the school and provides evidence as to why we are doing something. I am now able to think more carefully about implementing initiatives and take time to find out evidence about them first. (SENCO)

> It has brought a huge benefit to the quality of our teaching and learning. Each educational environment is different and undertaking research with our children, within the wider context of national and international research, has informed school teaching and learning policy. (Headteacher)

> Our SENCO's research has heightened staff and students' awareness of SEND issues and enhanced training for staff and governors. At our recent Ofsted, inspectors were glowing in their praise of this. (Headteacher)

It is essential that the profession becomes evidence and research based. We must have evidence of the impact on teaching and learning so pupils are not used as guinea pigs for untested interventions. (Headteacher)

Why is it important that teachers carry out research?

Teachers are immersed in the life of a school. Their deep involvement with teaching, learning and assessment places them in a strong position to influence outcomes for children. They have 'insider' knowledge and understanding that can enrich research investigations. With so much spent on education resources to enhance young people's education experiences, getting it right matters (The Royal Society 2018). Hattie (2016) argues that teachers need to determine what works and what doesn't – and, more importantly, know *why* something does or doesn't work. This is an important place for many teachers, especially SENCOs, to start their research and make a difference within their own context.

There can be tensions about what constitutes 'research'. Professional (academic) researchers often view their large-scale studies as 'real research' that is shared with a wide national/international audience, while teacher practitioner research can be dismissed as small-scale, anecdotal and non-replicable. I would challenge this view (as do other researchers like Nelson and O'Beirne 2014), because I think that smaller-scale research helps deepen understanding and relevance at a local level: it offers an opportunity to improve specific school practice and targeted students' educational experiences.

This is all important because if teachers don't engage with research several things could happen, as outlined below:

- The breadth of research evidence available will continue to fail to travel between those who carry it out and those who could benefit from it. Researchers have different priorities and produce conflicting results which may not be apparent when studies are disseminated to schools. Without this knowledge, it is hard for teachers to make informed decisions.
- Professional researchers will continue to dominate education research, and their results, which may exclude the deeper 'insider' perspectives of teachers and pupils, will continue to inform national policy.
- Busy teachers without time to critique research claims, might select strategies and interventions that promise much but have no solid evidence base, resulting in schools wasting significant money and

time. This is not helped by the 'information explosion' of variable quality available through the internet. Critically, in these situations, the cause of any lack of success may be placed on pupils – especially those with SEN – rather than the quality of the strategy or intervention, increasing their experiences of failure.

Will research make me a better teacher?

This is a question that I have often been asked by teachers and while I could not reassure any individual of this, I do know that reading about and carrying out research studies on issues that I really care about, has developed my practice and made me a better teacher. I was taught about critical reflection during my initial training, but only later learned how additional insights from research could help me challenge my practice. We should all be open to questioning ourselves, our practice, school policy and alternative viewpoints, and accept that involvement in research can be a challenging experience. When dealing with these challenges, I have found two factors within school environments to be important: trust and support from colleagues; and an enabling senior leadership team.

Education developments certainly seem to view teacher research as an important core activity for professional learning, with expectations of teachers becoming 'research literate' (EEF 2018, Evans et al. 2017, Cordingly 2015). Such expectations are seen within the Teachers' Standards and courses like the National Award for SEN Co-ordination and the National Leadership qualifications that now require participants to engage with research as part of their course activities. National funding of 'Research Schools' and school-led research projects also demonstrate significant movement towards raising the profile of teacher-initiated research and dissemination.

Gill Richards

This book

All of the authors in this book are practising SENCOs who carried out supervised individual research projects in their schools for their university courses. Through their accounts, they aim to share what they learned and explain the research processes they used to help readers understand how these can be replicated. Their investigations often involved small numbers or were conducted over a short period of time, so there is no attempt to make bold claims about their results. These SENCOs are hoping that by reporting on ways in which they made a difference in their own schools, this will inspire other teachers to use similar approaches.

Action research in schools benefits from including the views of everyone involved, especially the views of children, who are typical recipients of education developments and interventions. All of the SENCOs whose research involved support strategies ensured that teachers and children's perspectives were collected to inform and evaluate the strategies investigated. This good practice reflects an established approach used in Singapore, where schools have research groups comprising teachers *and* students.

Each chapter follows the same format. The school context is explained and why a specific strategy was selected for investigation. This is followed by details of the strategy and how evidence was collected. Impact of the strategy is then analysed and used to identify recommendations for practice.

The chapters

In Chapter 1, Katherine Chubb reports on a study in a primary school where there had been concern about measuring the impact of literacy and numeracy interventions on pupil achievement. A new system of continually monitoring interventions through a newly created observation quality framework and check sheets, supplemented with staff interviews and review of progress data, resulted in an increase in quality for these interventions. The chapter concludes with reflection on factors that can affect monitoring systems and recommendations for further development and reading resources.

In Chapter 2, Sorcha Walmsley reports on the trial of three new strategies to reduce anxiety and improve behaviour within a Year 6 class. The school had seen a large increase in children being identified with mental health difficulties, especially in relation to conditions of ADHD, autism and anxiety. The children were taught three strategies – deep-breathing, muscle relaxation and positive self-talk – with the aim of reducing instances of detention and periods of isolation, which were having a negative impact on learning. Evidence was collected over six months to assess the impact of these on their progress and attainment, and this is discussed to identify the positive effects on children's behaviour.

In Chapter 3, Maxine Siddall reports on how school feedback practice was developed to improve learning for pupils with SEN. The research project focused on reviewing the type and quality of marking and feedback given to pupils, and the impact it had on their progress. Evidence was collected through interviews with staff and pupils, scrutiny of planning and books, and a marking checklist. Recommendations are identified from this research for ways in which a whole school 'Marking and Feedback' policy can be developed that effectively meets the needs of all pupils.

In Chapter 4, Laura Inglis reports on the deployment of teaching assistants in a school with a high number of children identified as having special educational needs. Traditionally, TA support was delivered 1:1 outside of classrooms, but there had been doubts about the effectiveness of this and children were stating that they did not like to be separated from their peers. Information was collected from teachers, teaching assistants and pupils, and findings from this were used to design a new model of TA support which was successfully trialled for one term and evaluated. The chapter concludes with recommendations for ways in which the new model could be further developed.

In Chapter 5, Amy Breeze reports on a 'Quality First Teaching' professional development programme for a staff team to build their confidence in meeting the needs of students with SEN and become 'SEN Champions'. A baseline survey identified staff knowledge and confidence at the start, and this was used to plan targeted training with resources. A post-training questionnaire identified teachers had increased confidence in taking individual responsibility for meeting the needs of students with SEN and differentiating class work. The chapter concludes with recommendations for ways in which this model of professional development programme could be used to increase inclusive practice in school.

In Chapter 6, Lara Krause reports on a case study of three primary school classes that took part in a three-week daily 10-minute run around the school grounds, with the aim of providing an outlet for active behaviour and create a calmer classroom learning environment afterwards. Evidence was collected through questionnaires, analysis of 'behaviour incidents' and scrutiny of children's work. It was found that during the weeks in which the daily run took place, behaviour 'incidents' decreased by 30% for all children with ADHD and behavioural difficulties. The chapter concludes with recommendations for further developments of this approach and useful reading resources.

In Chapter 7, Rosemary Brooks reports on a secondary school's transition processes for pupils with SEN. It started from the school's concern that the needs of pupils might not be the same as those anticipated by staff. Surveys and interviews were carried out with pupils, parents and carers to discover their concerns about moving into secondary education. These identified which processes successfully supported transition from primary schools and where there had still been significant concerns. This led to new additional arrangements included within the school's transition and induction programmes. The chapter concludes with recommendations for further development of transition processes.

In Chapter 8, Jill Turner reports on a primary school's strategy to increase support for their significant number of children whose challenging behaviours had resulted in a high rate of exclusions. It introduced 'Key Adults' to be matched with children according to their needs, taking into account the children's views. This role provided support through meetings with their allocated child each day and acting as a 'bridge' between him/her and the teacher to aid full-time re-integration into the class. Observations, questionnaires and Boxall Profiles were completed to investigate the impact of this strategy: all children were successfully re-integrated into their classes. The chapter concludes by identifying key factors that had supported the process and how this strategy could be further developed.

In Chapter 9, Clare Bedford reports on a small rural primary school's development of termly audits to identify the level of resources and approaches used to meet the needs of pupils with SEN. An initial audit provided RAG ratings for each class and this was reviewed in regular follow-up audits to identify improvements. Good practice was shared between staff, and this, in addition to targeted developments, increased the quality of SEN support provision across all classrooms. The chapter concludes with recommendations for ways in which this approach can further support whole school development.

In Chapter 10, Katherine Smith reports on a case study of expectations placed on the SENCO role in response to the 'Special Educational Needs and Disabilities Code of Practice: 0–25 years' (2015). Data collected from 20 NASENCO graduates revealed the complexities of their roles within different settings, identifying the pressures they faced as mediators, negotiators, conflict resolvers and agents for change, often without relevant training for this. The chapter concludes with some useful practical recommendations about applying new procedures and development of new skills through training to support SENCOs in their increasingly complex role.

References

Cordingly, P. (2015) The contribution of research to teachers' professional learning and development, *Oxford Review of Education*, 41(2): 234–252

Education Endowment Foundation (EEF) (2018) *Annual Report 2018*, London: EEF

Evans, C., Waring, M. and Christodoulou, A. (2017) Building teachers' research literacy: integrating practice and research, *Research Papers in Education*, 32 (4): 403–423

Hattie, J. (2016) *Visible Learning into Action*, Abingdon: Routledge

Nelson, J. and O'Beirne, C. (2014) *Using evidence in the classroom: what works and why?* Slough: NfER

Ofsted (2019) *The Education Inspection Framework*, Manchester: Ofsted

The Royal Society (2018) *Harnessing Educational Research*. Available online at: www.royalsociety.org/education (Accessed on 27/06/19)

Chapter 1

The impact of introducing robust monitoring of interventions

Katherine Chubb

Context

My school is a smaller than average sized primary school and has a much lower than average proportion of pupils known to be eligible for free school meals. The proportion of pupils labelled as having Special Educational Needs and Disabilities (SEND) is below average, as is the proportion of pupils with an Education, Health and Care (EHC) plan. We run a number of Wave 2 and Wave 3 Literacy and Numeracy interventions, but as we have only 11 pupils on our SEND register, it is hard to obtain reliable data as to the effectiveness of the intervention programmes.

As a SEN Co-ordinator (SENCO), I have a key part to play in evaluating the impact of our provision on pupil progress. Indeed, the *Special Educational Needs and Disability Code of Practice: 0–25 Years* (2015) sets out that effective provision management can be used strategically to help a 'school to develop the use of interventions that are effective and to remove those that are less so' (DfE 2015: 6.77). I believed the systems in place in our school at the time were not rigorous enough and I wanted to investigate if there was a better system for monitoring and evaluating the impact of interventions which would enable me to link the outcomes of provision to performance management. This is a key step in moving from a system of provision mapping to provision management, as recommended by Gross (2015).

Through this research project I wanted to find out whether the quality of interventions could be improved by targeted training for those delivering them (Wearmouth 2016; Gross 2015). As our school systems stood, there was an overlap in responsibilities for professional development in our school, and for monitoring and evaluating the impact of interventions. Teaching Assistants (TAs) were at the time being observed once a year by a Higher Level Teaching Assistant (HLTA). The focus for these observations was decided upon by the Senior Leadership Team

(SLT) and based on targets from the School Development Plan, instead of using what research suggests – the quality features of an intervention session. The feedback given to those delivering interventions was not based around 'fidelity to the programme', which research by Gross (2015: 130) found to be highly important in terms of programme impact. Lack of school funding now means that there are fewer opportunities for accessing high quality training, but I would argue that a better understanding of expected intervention outcomes, within a system linked to performance management, could enable better targeting of funding for training where gaps in teacher and TAs' knowledge and skills have been identified.

Strategy

I narrowed my research to find out what impact introducing a more rigorous system for monitoring intervention sessions would have on the quality of the intervention and the progress made by the children involved in them. The system was to be based upon the 'fidelity' (the degree to which delivery protocols matched those intended by the programme authors) to each intervention programme. Feedback and training given would be linked to what research – such as that from The EEF Guidance Report (2017) on 'Improving Literacy in Key Stage 2' – suggests are the key quality features of an intervention session. The EEF Guidance Report (2015) into 'Making Best Use of Teaching Assistants' states that:

> At present there are only a handful of programmes in the UK for which there is secure evidence of effectiveness and if a school uses unproven interventions then we must ensure they include common elements of effective interventions … [we must] ensure there is fidelity to the programme and do not depart from suggested delivery protocols (EEF 2015: 24)

I identified four intervention programmes run in school where concerns had been raised by teachers and TAs as to their effectiveness, impact on progress and how closely we followed delivery protocols. The interventions included 'Number Box' (one child), 'Power of 2' (five children), 'Nessy Learning Programme' (five children) and 'Hornet Literacy Primer' (one child). These particular interventions do not appear on evidence rating system databases such as the online 'Evidence for Impact' (E4I) database (IEE n.d.), which highlights if there is secure evidence on the effectiveness on an intervention. It is also harder to collect reliable data on them, due to the small number of children taking part in them in our school.

With the consent of those delivering the interventions, I carried out two observations of each intervention programme delivered by TAs in school. Intervention sessions observed lasted from between 5 to 20 minutes in length. After the initial observation, I provided targeted feedback on how the quality of the session could be improved and carried out a follow-up observation seven weeks later. Before any observations took place, I produced check sheets that could be used as a basis for discussion around the 'fidelity to the programme' with the adults delivering the interventions. These check sheets contained:

- a summary of the delivery protocol for each intervention, with details on the aims of each programme
- the suggested target group, and
- further detail on the recommended length, frequency and assessment method.

I then researched the quality features of an effective intervention. I combined recommendations from the EEF Guidance Report (2015) with the format for an observation framework suggested by Gross (2015) and Wearmouth (2016). My observation framework (see Table 1.1) contained 22 quality features with prompts for the observer to help identify whether that feature was present in the intervention session being observed.

Collecting evidence to measure impact

Evidence collection

I chose to carry out observations of the four TAs delivering intervention sessions using the observation framework rather than questionnaires, because I aimed to 'bring certain practices and behaviours to light' and resolve any practical problems in the delivery of the intervention (Burton and Bartlett 2005: 114). This method also gave me quantitative data on the quality features of an intervention session observed before and after feedback was given to the adult delivering the programme. I was then able to analyse the results to see what impact the new system of monitoring had achieved.

Informed consent to be observed and interviewed as part of my research (which was additional to normal school practice) was gained from the TAs delivering the four identified interventions, and they were told they could opt out at any time (BERA 2018). I was aware that my research was taking place in a climate where there were concerns among TAs that their hours were at risk of being reduced. I made it clear to those who agreed to be involved that my research project was not in any way linked to this. I

Table 1.1 Observation framework

Observation framework quality features	_Observed in session_	_Evidence_
Are the right pupils targeted and are there clear entry and exit criteria for the intervention?		
Is the location appropriate?		
Is the frequency of the intervention as specified?		
Is the session length as specified in the programme?		
Does the session content match that specified in the programme?		
Are resources pre-prepared and are well managed?		
Do the adults know what the learning objectives are?		
Does the pupil know what the learning objectives are?		
Is the session planned and adjusted on the basis of assessment?		
Do pupils help identify their own learning targets and assess their own progress?		
Are key instructions and learning points given concisely and clearly and repeated as necessary?		
Is behaviour well managed and does the adult promote interaction between the pupils in the group or adult?		
Does the adult promote independence and help the pupil to recognise successful strategies helping them to apply them in other situations?		
Does the adult create a secure and supportive environment where there is safety to 'have a go' and make mistakes?		
Does the adult challenge the pupil and expect the most from them?		
Is the session active, lively and multisensory, with sessions being well paced?		
Does the class teacher review the intervention jointly?		
Does the class teacher and TA have time to meet to review pupil's progress?		
Is the pupil's progress carefully tracked?		
Has there been good training for the person delivering the curriculum?		
Are there opportunities for pupils to apply their learning and have it reinforced in class?		
Is parental involvement secured as specified in the programme?		

also made them aware that the observations were not to identify any individual's ability to deliver an intervention, but to investigate the effectiveness of the current systems in place for monitoring interventions. Children involved were identified as Child A (Number Box intervention), Child B (Nessy Learning Programme), Child C (Hornet Literacy Word Primer) and Child D (Power of 2 Maths Intervention). I also ensured that TAs' interview answers were anonymised (they were identified as TA1, TA2, TA3, TA4) and all research data was kept secure.

I then carried out an initial observation of TA1. I endeavoured to ensure that she felt at ease during the observation in order to minimise the impact my presence would have. From this observation, I identified a number of key features of an effective intervention that I could not observe within a session and would instead require interviews with the TAs involved after each observation. I developed an interview schedule to collect evidence to identify if the remaining quality features of the intervention were in place for that particular intervention programme. Questions asked were to elicit, for example, whether children got the opportunity to apply what they have been learning in the intervention to other contexts, and whether parents were informed about their child's involvement and progress in each intervention. In the second set of interviews, I did not stick as rigidly to the interview schedule. I took more of an unstructured approach so that interviewees were able to 'talk around the topic in their own way' and I could ask additional questions 'where a particular issue had not been covered' (Burton and Bartlett 2005: 95) to get more qualitative data.

Having carried out the initial observations and interviews, I provided feedback to each TA, referring to the relevant intervention check sheet. We then addressed any practical problems that had resulted in some of the intervention's quality features not being seen. Some TAs were not aware of individual's attainment data, so I collected this from the teachers who had overall responsibility for that child's progress. This enabled me to measure the impact that introducing a more rigorous system of monitoring had on the progress of the children involved in them.

Impact

One of the main findings from my observations and interviews can be seen in Figure 1.1. It shows that the number of quality features of an intervention session increased following the introduction of this more rigorous monitoring system. The average increase in the number of quality features observed was six, with the largest increase being nine.

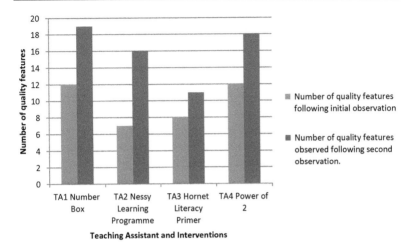

Figure 1.1 Chart comparing the number of quality features observed during the initial and second observation for each intervention

The impact that the new system of monitoring had on the progress of individuals involved in these interventions was mixed and while drawing any reliable conclusions was difficult due to the low number of children and the short time involved, I found that in all but the case of Child D, they had made progress. In particular, Child A, who was involved in the 'Number Box' intervention made progress with a gain of 15 months in her maths age in the seven-week period between observations and after the focused feedback given to TA1 (who delivered the intervention).

A key theme that arose during my research was that in the three out of the four interventions observed initially, the frequency that each child was taking part in them was different to that suggested by the intervention programme authors. TAs' interview responses supported this: when asked what was different about the way they delivered the intervention in comparison to the way it was intended, TA2 said 'timing' and TA4 said 'frequency'. The second interview with TA2 confirmed this:

> I knew they needed more sessions than they were getting, so I think it's nice then that they got five sessions, and all of them needed the five sessions, but like I said in the beginning, I think I have too many children, which is the problem.

The contents of the intervention check sheet, including the recommended frequency and duration for each particular intervention, was shared with both the TAs and teachers after the initial observation. The responses from my second set of interviews showed an improvement with all interventions delivered in line with the frequency and duration recommended by the intervention programme authors. Child B, who took part in the 'Nessy Learning Programme' made a gain of 12 points in his Maths Standardised Score. This compares with the average gain in the standardised score of four other children involved in the same intervention for only one session per week, which was 7.5. Although small numbers of children are involved, this supports the conclusions of the EEF report (2015) which states that effective intervention sessions should be 'brief (20–50 mins) and occur regularly (3–5) times per week' (EEF 2015: 5).

There was a very small increase in the number of quality features observed between intervention sessions for Child C, and she made limited progress. This may be linked to the amount and quality of the training received by the TA prior to my feedback. Further targeted training is needed to see if this would increase the number of quality features. If it did not, then this intervention programme may not be suitable for this child and may not be an effective intervention (the lowest number of quality features were seen in this intervention session).

Child D did not make progress and her point score gain dropped by 5 points. This is compared to four other children involved in the same intervention who made an average gain of 5.75 points. Child D had an unsettled home life during the period between the first observation to the second, which may account for this lack of progress.

The number of times that there was clear evidence to support that all resources were prepared in advance and well managed improved from three to four interventions. Following the observation of TA2, I was able to spot a practical problem where the TA was unable to hear the computer programme at the same time as the child, so I suggested the use of headphone splitters, which were then observed being used successfully during the second observation. I was also able to highlight the importance of knowing and sharing the learning objective when feeding back to the TAs. This follows recommendations from the EEF report (2015) that interventions should have clear objectives; all TAs took this feedback on board and it was evident in all four of the second observations. An appropriate location where there were fewer interruptions also improved in two of the four interventions observed.

Only one child in one session observed was given the opportunity to identify her own learning targets. My observations also found that there was no clear evidence that parental involvement was secured for any of the intervention sessions and this did not improve following feedback. I found that there was only an increase from one to two intervention sessions where there were opportunities for children to apply their learning and have it reinforced in class. This was the same for the number of intervention sessions where the TA felt there was time to meet with the teacher to review a child's progress.

Generally, the TAs had not received any extensive training from an experienced trainer or teacher. My results showed TA1 and TA4 were found to have the highest number of quality features in both the first and second observations. They had run the interventions for more than three years and had received training from TAs who had run the intervention before. The intervention that was observed to have the smallest increase in quality features was led by TA3, who said she had 'no training' on delivering this intervention.

It is impossible to draw reliable conclusions about whether the introduction of a more rigorous monitoring system had a positive impact on the progress of the children involved, due to the small sample of intervention sessions and the low number of other children involved. That said, the overall increase in the number of quality features does show that the more rigorous system had a positive impact on the quality of the intervention session being delivered. Originally, only two TAs felt they sometimes followed and delivered the programme in the way it was intended at the beginning of the project. After the feedback sessions, there was an improvement with all four TAs now indicating that they always followed the programme and delivered it in the way intended, reflecting EEF recommendations that the most effective interventions are where the TA 'closely follows the plan and structure of the intervention' (EEF 2015: 24).

Recommendations

Recommendations for practice

The ability to compare and monitor interventions by the number of quality features observed makes it much easier to identify which interventions are more effective (and ineffective) for individual children when reliance upon progress data is harder to monitor due to the low numbers involved in them.

Responses from TAs about the intervention check sheets were positive. TA2 felt that the check sheet was useful for developing their own practice when delivering the intervention and inferred they would be useful for teachers too, especially since the SEND Code of Practice (2015) clearly places the emphasis on teachers being responsible for the progress of all children in their class. My interviews highlighted a lack of awareness of the specific aims of individual intervention programmes, the progress that should be expected and how to secure parental involvement. In addition, the ability to make connections between out of class learning and classroom teaching only improved in one case and was only observed in two of the four second intervention sessions observed. In order to improve the quality of interventions and improve the extent to which interventions are implemented in line with the recommendations by the programme authors, I would advise that the intervention check sheets are shared with, and completed by, all staff. This would then maximise the impact of the interventions being run.

I would also recommend that in order to ensure that intervention provision is suitable for the needs of a child, teachers need an allotted time to discuss and review his/her progress jointly with the person delivering this. Ideally, teachers should also be more involved in observing the delivery of interventions and providing further training for those delivering them. 'Leading on Intervention' recommends 'joint planning and reviewing progress between teachers and teaching assistants', as this can ensure that learning from interventions is integrated into whole-class work where appropriate, and relevant links can be made (DfE 2010: 6). The EEF has now supplemented the 'Making Best Use of Teaching Assistants Guidance Report' (2015) with further resources available online to help schools to implement the recommendations made.

Through this project I have found that a robust system of monitoring makes it much easier to identify the quality features that are missing in a particular intervention and in the way it is being delivered. Regular monitoring is likely to result in staff taking greater care when planning and implementing interventions. If this new system were adopted, it would allow SENCOs to link the expected outcomes of provision to performance management more closely.

As mentioned previously, we had an overlap in responsibilities with professional development being led by two members of the Senior Leadership Team. The more robust monitoring system is labour intensive to set up initially, but I would argue the benefits outweigh this, as responsibilities could continue to be shared: this new system allows for observations of our interventions to still be carried out by other staff such as a HLTA or member of SLT, and information then easily shared with the SENCO. Results could be analysed alongside progress data and then fed back into performance management and professional development systems. Gaps or trends in the delivery of interventions by individuals could then be identified and addressed through the most appropriate form of CPD. Taking a 'collaborative approach' to continuing professional development is supported by NASEN who published guidance for

SENCOs following the findings of John Hattie's synthesis of international research (Hattie 2009), so our new system would be in line with their recommendations, with leaders able to jointly review 'current levels of expertise among staff and identify areas for development' (NASEN 2015: 7). As school budgets are tight and resources need to be used where they will have the greatest impact, a collaborative approach would take into account both the wider school improvement plan and school appraisal processes before planning a range of professional development opportunities to support school improvement.

Recommendations for reading

Burton, D. and Bartlett, S. (2005) *Practitioner Research for Teachers*, London: SAGE Publications.

This book provides useful guidance and discussion on the key issues to consider when designing and conducting practitioner research in school settings.

Education Endowment Foundation (2018) *Toolkit to Support Implementation of the Recommendations from the 'Making Best Use of Teaching Assistants Guidance Report'*. Available online at: https://educationendowm entfoundation.org.uk/tools/making-best-use-of-teaching-assistants

This is an online module that offers ideas, tools and guidance for schools and Senior Leadership Teams to help implement change and raise achievement within your own school context through consideration of the seven recommendations made in the EEF (2015) 'Making Best Use of Teaching Assistants Guidance Report'.

Gross, J. (2015) *Beating Bureaucracy in Special Educational Needs: Helping SENCOs Maintain a Work/Life Balance*, 3rd edn, Abingdon: Routledge

This book offers useful proformas that can be adapted to work within your own school context to help plan, monitor and evaluate your own provision for children with Special Educational Needs.

Wearmouth, J. (2016) *Effective SENCo. Meeting the Challenge*, Maidenhead: OUP

Helpful audits, observation tools and checklists can be found in this book to further develop and improve SEND provision within your own school.

References

BERA (2018) *Ethical Guidelines for Educational Research*, London: BERA
Burton, D. and Bartlett, S. (2005) *Practitioner Research for Teachers*, London: SAGE Publications

Department for Education (2010) Leading on Intervention: Managing the Work of Teaching Assistants. Available online at: https://webarchive.nationala rchives.gov.uk/20110813021146/http://nsonline.org.uk/node/41668 (Accessed 22/3/19)

Department for Education (2015) Special Educational Needs and Disability Code of Practice: 0–25 years. Available online at: www.gov.uk/government/publica tions/send-code-of-practice-0-to-25 (Accessed 22/3/19)

Education Endowment Foundation (2015) Making Best Use of Teaching Assistants Guidance Report. Available online at: https://educationendowm entfoundation.org.uk/tools/guidance-reports/making-best-use-of-teaching-a ssistants (Accessed 3/3/19)

Education Endowment Foundation (2017) Improving Literacy in Key Stage 2 Guidance Report. Available online at: https://educationendowmentfoundation. org.uk/tools/guidance-reports/literacy-ks-2/ (Accessed 14/4/19)

Gross, J. (2015) *Beating Bureaucracy in Special Educational Needs: Helping SENCOs Maintain a Work/Life Balance*, 3rd edn, Abingdon: Routledge.

Hattie, J. (2009) *Visible Learning. A Synthesis of Over 800 Meta-analyses Relating to Achievement*, Abingdon: Routledge

Institute for Effective Education (n.d.) Evidence for Impact (E4I) Database. Available online at: www.evidence4impact.org.uk/index.php (Accessed 14/4/19)

NASEN (2015) Collaborative Learning for SEN: The Role of the SENCO. Available online at: www.nasen.org.uk/resources/resources.collaborative-lea rning-for-sen-the-role-of-the-senco.html (Accessed 14/4/19)

Wearmouth, J. (2016) *Effective SENCo. Meeting the Challenge*, Maidenhead: OUP

Does embedding anxiety-reducing strategies in the classroom improve behavioural and educational outcomes for children in Year 6?

Sorcha Walmsley

Context

Our school is a larger than average primary school and 93% of our school population live in households at the two highest bands of deprivation for both IDACI (Income Deprivation Affecting Children Index) and IMD (Index of Multiple Deprivation). Children who attend our school have multiple barriers to their learning, ranging from lack of support at home and low aspirations, to poor health, nutrition and behavioural issues. As a result of rigorous baselining and moderation with other schools, we know that our children begin school in Reception with very low starting points. Our main feeder nursery school is an Enhanced Resource Nursery for additional needs and these children join our mainstream provision. The percentage of pupils eligible currently for pupil premium funding is 60% (at the last census) which is a significant reduction from previous years. All of these factors contribute towards many of our children having diffi-culty managing their social and emotional needs, regardless of whether they have any special educational needs.

There are currently 66 children on our SEND (Special Educational Needs and Disability) register; five have an EHCP (Education, Health and Care Plan) and there are nine on the monitoring register. Of the 66 children on the SEND register, 43 have some difficulty with Social, Emotional and Mental Health (SEMH), although this might not be their only need. We have nurture groups and interventions that are having a positive impact on supporting children with some social and emotional difficulties. However, one area for which we have limited interventions or support is mental health and well-being. Hackett (2018) informs us that half of all life-time mental health issues emerge before the age of 14 and I have noticed recently that on the paper work we are receiving from doctors, diagnoses of 'Anxiety' have become more common. We have had six children diagnosed with anxiety this academic year, compared to none previously while I have been SENCO (since November 2015).

Masia Warner et al. (2013) stated that ensuring strategies to support social anxiety are taught within school may effectively support children who would otherwise not access services. Mindful of this, I decided to teach and embed three anxiety-reducing techniques that children could implement: progressive muscle relaxation, deep-breathing exercises and positive self-talk. I selected for this a group of 25 Year 6 children that I teach for Literacy. Within this group, there are four children with ADHD and/or Autism (one of whom is also at risk of exclusion), one child at risk of permanent exclusion for refusal behaviour and one child with a diagnosis of anxiety – all of which are on the SEND register for SEMH difficulties. My research predominantly focused on them, although the strategies were taught to the whole class. This was to help develop an inclusive approach rather than highlight the children's difficulties. A general letter was sent to the Literacy set's parents to inform them of a new strategy being implemented within school and consent was requested for the six children to take part in the research element.

Strategy

The three anxiety-reducing techniques that I introduced were progressive muscle relaxation, deep-breathing exercises and positive-self talk. The main focus of their implementation into lessons was to see if the children could adopt these techniques effectively to lessen work avoidance and disruptive behaviours. This would result in them not leaving the lessons and missing out on their learning time. It was my aim that by increasing the children's time in class, their progress, achievement and enjoyment within lessons would improve.

Positive muscle relaxation

This uses the premise that mental calmness can be achieved through physical relaxation (Stoppler 2019). The children would tense a muscle group (e.g. neck muscles) and contract them for 10 seconds before exhaling and relaxing the muscles. They then worked down their bodies, repeating the process with the next muscle group until arriving at their feet. Alongside this, the children listened to relaxing music. This was introduced as a whole class activity to start lessons and encourage everyone to feel relaxed – it was particularly effective for lessons that happened straight after playtimes.

Deep breathing exercises

According to LaLande et al. (2011), deep-breathing techniques can be used to control feelings of anxiety. For this, the children inhaled through their nose and exhaled through their mouths to increase oxygen levels in the body and give them something to focus on other than the cause of their anxiety. They tried this in a variety of positions – lying down, sitting in chairs, sitting on the floor … wherever they felt most comfortable – to ensure they could use their hands to feel their abdominal muscles rising and falling as they breathed in and out. After introducing this technique, the children were left to use it whenever they needed to, but were encouraged to use it by their peers and myself if any of us could see them becoming distressed.

Positive self-talk (PST)

Treadwell and Kendall (1996) found that students who had been given opportunities to replace negative self-talk with positive self-talk could identify and discuss triggers to their anxiety, and positive self-talk had long-term benefits to their general health. So, we started by asking the children to identify some of the things that they think when they are worried or anxious. We then spent time discussing how their thoughts could be changed to become more positive – for example: 'I can't do this' might become 'What do I need to help me be able to do this?'. They then made posters and flip-books with their positive phrases in them. The children started by saying the phrases to a partner and then to themselves when they realised that they were thinking negatively. Their peers also reminded them to use PST when they heard them speaking negatively. We spent a session learning about PST and creating the posters and flip-books, which they referred to throughout the following months.

Collecting evidence to measure impact

Evidence collection

I decided to use a mixed method approach, because this 'opens the door' to different views, assumptions, forms of data collection and analysis (Creswell 2016: 11). Due to the small sample size, I wanted to use a qualitative approach to ensure that I could analyse the potential impact of the anxiety-reducing activities on individual's achievement and behaviour. So, my mixed methods involved the use of qualitative and quantitative research methods to triangulate my results and improve reliability and validity.

As with all research, it was important to consider the ethical issues that may arise in line with the British Educational Research Association's guidelines (2018). I ensured that I gained consent from the parents and guardians of all participants to complete the research, use pictures of their child and any data collected. I also received permission from the headteacher and parents to interview the children. Confidentiality and anonymity were maintained at all times: all of the children's names were changed and referred to by initials.

I was aware that there is often an imbalance of authority when completing research with children, with adults deciding if a child participates. I wanted to avoid this and ensure that the children were given a choice. I explained to them, prior to implementing the strategies, what we were planning on doing and the aims of the intervention. I then gained their consent to use examples of work, pictures, observations and quotes from discussions during the following weeks. They were clearly excited and all of them wanted to take part. I broke the permission areas into small criteria to ensure that the children could see what kinds of information I was planning to gather, and we discussed these and how the information might be used. When all consent had been obtained, I began my action research project.

My project used one main qualitative research method – semi-structured interviews with the focus group of six children. As many have argued (e.g. Swaminathan and Mulvihill 2017), interviewing is not just an exchange of questions and answers; some form of empathy between the interviewer and interviewees is required. Mindful of this, I interviewed the children because I had a good relationship with them – I had been their class teacher twice during their time at school and, as SENCO, had previously supported them in managing their needs in school.

I used a semi-structured group interview with the children to encourage group interaction and participation, and because it is often less intimidating than individual interviews. It also enabled me to delve deeper into information if required. The interview questions comprised some closed-questions, but the majority were open-ended. I followed guidance by established researchers (Thomas 2017) that included: 1) preparing the interview schedule using prompts and equivalent time to ensure equal coverage of questions; and 2) providing opportunities for 'conversations' to develop so that all participant views are well represented. The questions focused around how effective they found the strategies and we reflected on times where they had used them, or not, and why they thought that was. I finished the interview by asking the children about what they thought their next steps should be.

For my quantitative research methods, I decided to use a Boxall Profile to identify if the strategies had a positive impact upon the children's social and emotional well-being – this, Bennathan and Boxall (1998) argue, provides objective data to support teachers' intuitive judgements. I also decided to track each child's behaviour profile using 'Otrack' – our school's behaviour monitoring system – and as the children were in Year 6, I used the interim framework and standardised scaled scores developed in school to track each child's individual progress and attainment.

I started by collecting some baseline data so that any progress was measurable and any individual starting points and gaps could be identified. Before introducing the anxiety reducing strategies, I completed a Boxall assessment for all six children at the end of the autumn term. I involved the class teaching assistant (TA) in doing this, to increase accuracy because she saw the children in other circumstances outside of the classroom. This profile enabled me to identify starting points for addressing some of the emotional and behavioural difficulties the children were displaying. I then repeated this assessment at the end of the year to identify if any progress had taken place.

Impact

The baseline information showed that most of the children displayed high-level and low-level behaviours, both within lessons and outside – see Table 2.1. I grouped their behaviours that resulted in missed learning time into four areas: refusal, disrespect, physical/verbal abuse and exclusions.

I also collected their end of year attainment levels for Year 5; these are marked with E (emerging), M (met) or X (exceeding). The number represents the school year that they are working within (a child is expected to make a minimum of one year's progress within the year).

Our school has developed a standardised scoring sheet using SATs tests and sample tests (SATs and CGP). Using the scores achieved in the September results, 12 points are added to show expected progress: all children are expected to score 100 on the scaled test by the end of Year 6. Table 2.2 shows the children's predicted attainment data.

The children's initial Boxall Profiles showed five to be at risk developmentally and diagnostically, and the other at risk diagnostically. Some of the key areas that showed a developmental need were: 'accommodating others' and 'is biddable and accepts constraints', and within the diagnostic section: 'self-negating', 'shows inconsequential behaviour', 'insecure sense of self' and 'shows negativism towards self and others'.

Table 2.1 Behaviours resulting in missed learning time

Child	Baseline behaviours: June Year 5 – November Year 6			
	Refusal	Disrespect	Physical/verbal abuse	Exclusions
OB	14	16	27	0
BC	18	9	14	3
RH	15	4	8	1
JS	1	0	0	0
CP	24	5	2	1
LP	31	17	19	6

Table 2.2 Expected progress and predicted attainment

Child	R = Reading, W = Writing, M = Maths											
	End of Year 5 assessments			Prediction for end of Year 6			Sept baseline standardised score			Prediction for SATs results		
	R	W	M	R	W	M	R	W	M	R	W	M
OB	M5	E5	M5	M6	E6	M6	93	88	92	105	100	104
BC	X4	X3	E4	X5	X4	E5	70	77	78	82	99	90
RH	M5	E5	E6	M6	E6	X6	89	83	90	101	105	102
JS	M5	M5	M5	M6	M6	M6	88	90	90	100	102	102
CP	M5	E5	E6	E6	E6	X6	91	90	91	103	102	103
LP	E3	E3	X3	E4	E4	X4	70	79	76	82	91	88

Within the group interview, some interesting findings became apparent. The children enjoyed learning about the different techniques: "They have been really interesting …" (LP) and "The strategies, particularly positive self-talk and deep breathing, have helped me" (JS). CP was the only child to suggest that she had found the strategies "useful sometimes". As the interview progressed, it became clear that all of the children had more success using the strategies inside, rather than outside, the classroom.

All of the children felt that the techniques had helped them to succeed in multiple ways during the year. The main focus was on behavioural improvements and they could see the link between improving and managing their behaviours and how that led to improved attainment. Children identified that by implementing the deep-breathing, relaxation and positive self-talk, they were able to manage their behaviours better, resulting in them attending more lessons and succeeding academically more than they had expected:

I have been surprised at how much easier everything has got. I don't get into trouble as much so people are nicer to me and the lessons have been loads easier because I have been there! (OB)

I am also proud that I have not missed a morning lesson due to my behaviour this year. I think because I was able to stay in class more, I learnt more! (LP)

The interview also highlighted on numerous occasions how the children's perceptions of their ability to persevere with given tasks had improved:

Sometimes I wanted to give up, but the strategies, particularly positive self-talk and deep breathing, have helped me. (JS)

By the end, I am not as cross as I was and can always finish my work. (CP)

I also won the 'Writing Champion' pen this term as I have completed all of my writing and did not give up, even when it was hard. (RH)

Another finding was that for JS, a child whose behaviour was not necessarily limiting him from accessing his learning, the strategies had helped him socially. He noted, "but I feel that I have made some good friends this year which I haven't done before" and "I think I'm liked more by people".

Finally, five of the children suggested that 'next steps' should include sharing information about the three techniques in a variety of forms. They identified that deep breathing, relaxation and positive self-talk had helped them in a range of ways, and that sharing this may help them to succeed more and adults to understand better. JS suggested that it would be beneficial to share the information with midday supervisors after hearing some of the children's difficulties at lunch, "Maybe the dinner ladies could learn about the strategies so they could help people by reminding them of relaxation and deep breathing in particular" and CP suggested, "We could do an assembly about the different strategies and have everyone in school use them."

After nine months, when the children had embedded the strategies into every day practice, I analysed each child's attainment and progress scores and compared them to their predicted scores. Table 2.3 shows a summary of their results – all of the children either met or exceeded their predictions from the end of Year 5, except RH in Maths who achieved a one micro-band below his prediction. All children met or exceeded their SATs prediction.

When I compared the children's behaviour reports, they had all reduced their incidents of the four behaviours – see Table 2.4. Refusal behaviour started as the most common behaviour that resulted in them missing learning time. By July, the most common behaviour that resulted in missed sessions was physical and/or verbal abuse (although these

Table 2.3 Summary of results

Child	R = Reading, W = Writing, M = Maths											
	Prediction for end of Year 6			Actual end of Year 6 assessment			Prediction for SATs results			Actual SATs score		
	R	W	M	R	W	M	R	W	M	R	W	M
OB	M6	E6	M6	M6 +	M6	M6	105	100	104	112	113	107
BC	X5	X4	E5	E6	E6	E6	82	99	90	103	99	101
RH	M6	E6	X6	M6	M6	M6	101	105	102	107	105	108
JS	M6	M6	M6	M6 +	M6	M6	100	102	102	105	108	107
CP	M6	E6	X6	M6	M6	M6 +	103	102	103	108	111	110
LP	E4	E4	X4	E6	E6	E6	82	91	88	97	98	99

Table 2.4 Reduced incidents of the four behaviours

Child	Behaviours: November Year 6 – July Year 6							
	Refusal		Disrespect		Physical/verbal abuse		Exclusions	
	Pre-Nov	Dec – July	Pre Nov	Dec – July	Pre Nov	Dec – July	Pre Nov	Dec – July
OB	14	3	16	5	27	8	0	0
BC	18	10	9	5	14	12	3	1
RH	15	2	4	2	8	7	1	0
JS	1	0	0	0	0	0	0	0
CP	24	5	5	1	2	1	1	0
LP	31	9	17	5	19	7	6	0
Total reduction of incidents	103–29 = 74 less incidents		51–18 = 33 less incidents		70–35 = 35 less incidents		11–1 = 10 less incidents	

incidents had halved overall). This behaviour was not happening in the classroom, but was occurring during playtimes and lunchtimes, and as a consequence, was following through into the next sessions.

The Boxall Profile findings showed that over the nine months where the strategies were implemented and embedded, all children made improvements within their developmental and diagnostic strands overall. Some trends that I noticed are listed below:

1   The section 'T', which shows inconsequential behaviour, saw large-scale reductions (between 5–9 points), or the children who already scored low on the initial assessment had reduced it to 0.
2   Within the section 'X – shows negativism towards self', despite significant individual reductions (between 4–9 points less), this was still an area for which all the focus children were functioning at a considerably higher level than a 'neuro-typical child'.
3   One area that had limited improvement from all children was 'E – engages cognitively with peers'.

Recommendations

Recommendations for practice

It is clear from my research findings that the children made progress academically, behaviourally and within their developmental and diagnostic strands of the Boxall Profile. The findings highlighted some important points that have led to three recommendations.

First, during the interview, several children (between four and six) identified that although they felt the techniques had helped them within class, it was increasingly difficult to manage them outside. This was reflected in the number of sessions still missed due to physical/verbal abuse, compared to greater reductions seen in other areas of behaviour. Briggs suggests that strategies are easier for children to implement in the classroom due to the familiarity and structure of situations and that 'problems also arise because of misunderstandings between pupils' (Briggs 2012: 107). Having analysed the Boxall Profile assessments, one trend that seemed to occur throughout the children's profiles was their difficulty to engage cognitively with peers. Again, this would suggest that although the techniques had benefits in supporting children within classrooms, they had not helped in situations where there was limited adult support (such as during playtimes). In the group interview, children identified that they felt "too excited" and "forgot", so to ensure the benefits could be transferred beyond the classroom, it would be good to have signs made for outside the classroom and a buddy-system created, where children could remind each other to use the techniques.

Another point for consideration is that some of the children were in my class as well as in my literacy group: other children, like BC and RH were only in my literacy group – both of whom mentioned finding it difficult to recall the techniques. Although they had made progress with their behaviours and associated incidents, they had not reduced them as much as the others. It would be interesting to discover whether children felt more comfortable using the techniques in the classroom where they learned them and if I had been more inclined to encourage them to use these rather than letting their behaviours escalate, whereas their own class teachers may not have done that? Dean (2016) noted that children often want to please adults and gain extrinsic recognition. Although all staff members were informed of the strategies we were implementing, it is likely that in a classroom where the children can seem to 'please' the adult leading particular strategies, they may use them more. Dean (2016) also argued that intrinsic rewards were more satisfactory. I would like to embed these techniques as a whole-school approach so that all children can be supported in similar ways and reminded of the approaches. With time, and with the children seeing their own improvements, I would hope they would start to intrinsically reward themselves for their accomplishments.

The next steps for our school is to share the findings with the Intervention Teachers and TAs who run specific sessions to support children with SEMH difficulties and implement a seamless whole-school approach within all classrooms and wider activities. The evidence collected showed the improvements children can make socially, emotionally, behaviourally and academically. I also now want to ensure that our other interventions for SEMH have a more robust tracking system so that we can be assured of children's progress in their behaviour and achievements.

Finally, if you want to implement this project into your schools, I would recommend ensuring that all staff members are informed about it, particularly staff who support the children during unstructured times. It would be useful to develop a consistent language when discussing the strategies so that it is familiar and quick for the children to recall what they should do. It will need to work alongside your current behaviour management systems. It is not meant to replace anything that you have in schools, but I have found it to work effectively in reducing the children's escalations of behaviours and has been used as a preventative intervention more than a cure. I wish you the best in any endeavour to support children with their mental health and anxiety, and hope that it is as successful in your settings as it has been in ours.

Recommendations for reading

Gosch, E.A., Flannery-Schroeder, E., Mauro, C.F. and Compton, S.N. (2006) Principals of cognitive-behavioral therapy for anxiety disorders in children, *Journal of Cognitive Psychotherapy*, 20(3): 247–262.

This article shares some strategies that could be implemented in classrooms to support children and their anxiety.

Masia Warner, C., Brice, C., Esseling, P.G., Stewart, C.E., Mufson, L. and Herzig, K. (2013) Consultants' perceptions of school counselors' ability to implement an empirically-based intervention for Adolescent Social Anxiety Disorder, *Administration and Policy in Mental Health and Mental Health Services Research*, 40(6): 541–554.

This article provides some insightful reading into the importance of education in supporting children with their mental health, suggesting that educational practitioners and settings could be in the best position to implement interventions.

References

Bennathan, M. and Boxall, M. (1998) *The Boxall Profile Handbook*, London: The Nurture Group Network

British Educational Research Association (BERA) (2018) *Ethical Guidelines for Educational Research*, London: BERA

Briggs, S. (2012) *Inclusion and How to Do It*, London: Routledge

Cresswell, J. (2016) *Research Design: Qualitative, Quantitative, and Mixed Methods Approaches*, London: Sage Publications

Dean, J. (2016) *Organising Learning in the Primary School Classroom*, 4th edn, Abingdon: Routledge

Hackett, K. (2018) Will the green paper transform mental health services for children and young people? *Mental Health Practice*, 22(1): 8–10

LaLande, L., Bambling, M., King, R. and Lowe, R. (2011) Breathwork: An additional treatment option for depression and anxiety? *Journal of Contemporary Psychotherapy*, 42: 113–119

Masia Warner, C., Brice, C., Esseling, P., Stewart, C., Mufson, L. and Herzig, K. (2013) Consultants' perceptions of school counselors' ability to implement an empirically-based intervention for Adolescent Social Anxiety Disorder, *Administration and Policy in Mental Health and Mental Health Services Research*, 40(6): 541–554

Stoppler, M. (2019) *Progressive Muscle Relaxation for Stress and Insomnia*. Available online at: www.medicinenet.com/progressive_muscle_relaxation/views.htm (Accessed 01/03/19)

Swaminathan, R. and Mulvihill, T. (2017) *Critical Approaches to Questions in Qualitative Research*, Oxen: Routledge

Thomas, G. (2017) *How to Do Your Research Project*, London: Sage

Treadwell, K.R. and Kendall, P.C. (1996) Self-talk in youth with anxiety disorders: States of mind, content specificity, and treatment outcome, *Journal of Consulting and Clinical Psychology*, 64(5): 941–950

Chapter 3

A marked improvement for pupils with special educational needs and disabilities

Maxine Siddall

Context

My research took place in a large junior school with 250 pupils on roll. It is located in an ex-mining village within a socially deprived area. The proportion of pupils with Special Educational Needs and Disabilities (SEND) is 28.5%, which is higher than the national average, as is the number of pupils entitled to additional funding through the pupil premium.

I completed an audit of current SEND practice in school and identified a need to improve the feedback and marking given to pupils with SEND to develop their learning. The audit highlighted many questions that I wanted to investigate, and this is what formed my action research plan.

Strategy

Feedback is a vital tool in the promotion of pupil progress and key to teaching pupils effectively. The role feedback plays in achievement has been the focus of much contemporary pedagogical debate and there is emerging literature, which I have found useful while undertaking this research project.

Researchers Wilson (2012) Hattie and Timperley (2007) and the findings in the EEF (2016) suggest that it isn't always the giving of feedback that causes learning gains, it is the acting on feedback that determines how much pupils learn, and the following points should be considered:

- What feedback describes is the key to its impact.
- Feedback that directs attention to the intended learning has a positive impact on achievement.
- Feedback is most effective when it points out strengths in the work and gives guidance for improvement.

Marking is a central part of a teacher's role and is integral to progress and attainment. This is supported by the Education Endowment Foundation (EEF), which stated that written responses are a key way of providing feedback to pupils and help teachers assess their understanding, but ineffective marking was pointless and did not help pupils with SEND improve their learning (EEF 2016). The Independent Teacher Workload Review Group (2016) also found that there is no one-size-fits-all approach and a balance needs to be struck between a consistent approach and trusting teachers to focus on what is best for their pupils and circumstances.

I wanted to explore the effectiveness of written and verbal feedback given to pupils with SEND, and the impact this had on their progress and achievement. The project focused on the type and quality of the feedback given, pupils' ability to act upon it and progress. This information would be used to make recommendations for further developing our school's practice.

Collecting evidence to measure impact

Evidence collection

Evidence collection involved teachers, teaching assistants and 55 pupils identified as having SEND across all year groups. Interviews were conducted with ten Year 3 and Year 4 pupils who had a range of SEND. They were selected so that the impact of our current policy could be measured over a longer period of attendance in school and would experience any changes implemented after the research study. I also collected evidence from pupil questionnaires, a staff meeting, work scrutinises, English lesson planning and our marking policy.

First, I devised a pupil questionnaire to discover their experiences of feedback. This was discussed and amended with the head teacher. This questionnaire could be used with all pupils in the school but for the purpose of my action research, it was just given to all 55 pupils with SEND. A member of staff went through each question with the pupils to clarify misunderstandings. This was undertaken in groups or on a 1:1 basis. I analysed the data and summarised the key findings. I then undertook the following:

- Reviewed a selection of books from pupils with SEND to identify whether marking was effective, consistent throughout school, adhered to the current marking policy; and if pupils had made a response to the feedback given.

- Made a selection of ten pupils with SEND from Years 3 and 4 and discussed the marking in their books and the feedback that they received.
- Held a staff meeting where the focus was to discuss marking and feedback and I noted staff responses.
- Reviewed our school marking policy, noting that it was a 'marking' policy and reference to feedback was absent.
- Reviewed a selection of planning from Years 3, 4 and 5 to see if feedback opportunities and time to act upon it were planned into English lessons.

Finally, after collecting all the evidence, I completed a 'marking checklist' to address where we were currently as a school. This checklist involved questions from the NASEN (2018) guidance about what Ofsted would consider when making a judgement on whether pupils with SEND understood how to improve their learning as a result of useful feedback (written or oral) from teachers.

Ethical procedures (BERA 2018) were followed when asking pupils to complete the questionnaires and take part in interviews. The pupils were asked if they agreed to fill in the questionnaires, talk with me about the marking in their books and if they felt comfortable for me to share their views with other members of staff. All of the pupils were happy to do so bar one, who became anxious, so I stopped the discussion and he went back to class. Staff consented to me looking at books and taking part in the staff discussion, as they felt it would improve current practice. All of the data and information gathered was stored confidentially and discussions were held with the headteacher about what appropriate information should be shared with staff.

Impact

All the information I gathered provided me with a clear overview of what we need to address as a school to improve current practice. My findings have led to the conclusion that this action research is not the small-scale project I anticipated it to be: there are many improvements and changes that must be made to our current practice, which will need to be measured termly over the course of the academic year.

Pupil responses from the discussions and questionnaires

It was clear from the questionnaires and pupil discussions that pupils understood why teacher comments were written in green and pink.

Thirty-three of the 55 pupils said they preferred written feedback as opposed to 20 who preferred verbal feedback. The remaining pupils didn't have a preference. More than half of the pupils said that they liked reading the feedback. Their responses included the following:

"It helps me to understand what I've done good."
"They help me to learn from my mistakes."
"I can write back to the comment."
"I like to know what I've done good at."
"Makes me understand what I have done wrong."
"I don't like reading them because there is always something bad."
"Because the teacher puts a word or phrase that I don't understand ... sometimes can't
read it and it scares me because it might be good or bad."
"Sometimes I can't read what the teacher has written, or it takes too long."
"It's boring, means I have to do more writing."

The pupils who didn't like reading their feedback nearly all referred to 'pink' comments as 'bad'. This was worrying and needs to be addressed immediately as no child should feel that their work is 'bad': it brings a sense that their efforts and what they have produced is not valued.

Only 13 of the 55 pupils understood the comments that were written, while 18 didn't understand any of them and 24 were unsure. It would appear from these findings that 42 pupils were unclear about the comments written, yet 33 pupils originally said they preferred written feedback when asked. This could suggest that they would prefer written feedback if they understand the comments more and the systems used. Their reasons for not understanding written feedback were that: teachers used words they didn't understand; the comments were too long and they couldn't read them; and they really didn't understand what they had to do, especially for comments like 'Use paragraphs', when they didn't know what a paragraph was. One pupil said, "If I see lots of green and pink writing, I just don't read it as it puts me off!" Some pupils suggested that it was helpful when the teacher gave them an example.

It was clear that pupils associated green as 'good' and they knew they had done well. What some of them didn't understand was why words or phrases were highlighted in green, suggesting that 'green' comments were not associated with learning objectives. Overall, it appeared that 29 of the 55 pupils did not really understand how to improve their work. Several said that they preferred to talk to the teacher about their work as it was then explained to them clearly and they could ask more questions if they still didn't understand. This supports the findings of the EEF (2016), which identified that engagement in dialogue led to pupils becoming more reflective about their work.

Nearly half of the pupils said they did not have enough time to respond to marking and only a few said they responded to comments made: opportunities to respond seemed to be a starter activity in a morning, at the end of a lesson, once a week or "when we get chance". Pupils said they would like more time to respond to comments and they would find it useful if it could be done shortly after it was given. It was clear that unless time is set aside for pupils to consider written comments, it is unlikely that our teachers are maximising the impact of their marking completed out of class time.

Some pupils said that seeing lots of writing at the end of their work "put them off" reading it and they would prefer comments to be shorter or more visual, like stamps or stickers. Research by the EEF (2016) showed that there was no difference between the effectiveness of coded or uncoded feedback, provided that pupils understand what the codes mean. However, the use of generic targets may make it harder to provide precise feedback and that is something we will need to consider.

It was evident from the pupils' questionnaires that they did not recognise verbal feedback or 'live' marking, and had little opportunity to peer mark and self-assess their work against a checklist. They were not always clear what the learning objectives were for lessons and said it would be helpful to have these stuck or written in their books.

Book scrutiny

Reviewing the pupils' books was valuable as it gave an overview of the marking undertaken and feedback given by teachers, and the level of response from pupils. It showed that our marking policy was not consistently applied across school or year groups. Teachers made comments in green to indicate what pupils had done well, but this was not always linked to a learning objective. This could, as Chappuis (2015) suggests, make pupils believe that finishing, rather than learning, is the goal of their effort. Some green comments were not specific enough – for example, the statement 'You have some good sentences here' did not tell the pupil which were good or why. Similarly, pink comments such as 'We will practice editing together next time' were not specific enough, nor did they always allow for pupils to be able to improve their own work.

The review also highlighted the need for examples to be given to some pupils so they could gain a better understanding of what is asked of them. A target that says 'Add some describing words' is meaningless to children if they are not sure what a 'describing word' is. Pupils are also asked in targets to 'think' about something – with a comment like, 'You need to think about the punctuation you should use.' It would be better for the teacher to ask them a more specific question about where and which punctuation could have been used. In some pupils' books, words and phrases were highlighted but the comments as to why were sometimes written at the end of the work; others were written in the margin and some lacked a comment to say why a particular word or phrase was good.

Abbreviations were not used consistently. Some teachers used 'sp', 'p' and 'gr' in the margin and then underlined the words with the mistakes. Others did not use them at all, but just corrected the mistakes. If we as teachers always highlight or correct the 'mistake' it does not really allow the pupil to think for themselves, nor deepen their learning because the teacher is doing it for them.

Some pupils initialled work to show they had read teachers' comments, but it was not clear whether they understand them or have been given the opportunities to act upon them. Comments made in pink seemed to focus repeatedly for some pupils on the same point. If these comments are continually being made, then it suggests that some additional teaching is required to address the target rather than continually telling the child to improve it. Feedback can only build on learning: if the learning isn't there, the feedback isn't going to move it forward.

Staff responses from the feedback and marking meeting

The Independent Teacher Workload Review Group (DfE 2016) noted that written marking had become unnecessarily burdensome for teachers and recommended that all marking should be driven by professional judgement and be meaningful, manageable and motivating: it was this that formed the basis of the staff meeting discussion.

On average, teachers in our school spent between 2 and 3 hours each week marking English and topic books. An average of 10–20 minutes per week was allocated for pupils to respond to the feedback. Peer feedback was not used regularly, and verbal feedback tended to be given to pupils whose work was difficult to read, or who had not completed the task well. Teachers did occasionally 'live' mark with a child and said they would like to do this more, but time was an issue.

The targets that are on the support plans of pupils with SEND were not referred to when work was being completed and marked, apart from in a Year 3 class where the pupils had these in front of them when writing. They were given a sticker to put on their chart if they showed elements of this in their written task. A way to improve this would be to make a comment in the marked piece of work too as evidence.

It was clear that there was a lack of time given to pupils to respond to marking, compared to the amount of time teachers spend marking. There was opposition to changing practice from some staff who felt that they were following policy and it worked well, but generally staff did agree that the marking of work and the feedback given to pupils with SEND was not always effective.

Recommendations

Recommendations for practice

There was a valuable amount of information that emerged from the action research that we can implement to improve our current practice in school. The marking policy must be a priority as it needs updating in line with my findings. As part of this, we need to consider whether our policy puts the 'hard work' on the teacher or the learner.

Other recommendations include the following.

Written feedback:

- Give pupils *regular* opportunities to respond to written comments.
- Give pupils with SEND more time to respond to marking.
- Consider simplifying written comments and use of language.
- Refer to targets on Support Plans of pupils with SEND.
- Make notes for teaching assistants so they can feed back effectively and know which steps pupils with SEND need to take to improve their work.
- Mark against the learning objective of the lesson.
- Ensure there is a balance of green and pink comments.
- Ensure green comments are specific about what the child has achieved.
- Ensure pink comments are targets that the pupils can act upon to improve their understanding and learning.
- Use stamps/symbols for pupils with SEND in relation to hand-writing, punctuation and grammar to eliminate the need for some written comments.

Other types of feedback:

- Verbal feedback should happen regularly, especially for pupils with SEND who may struggle to read and understand written comments.

It must involve the use of questions to judge the pupils' understanding and steer the learning process.

- 'Live' marking alongside pupils should take place so that they are encouraged to find mistakes with prompting and questioning and 'learn for themselves'.
- Peer marking should be used regularly. Rules to be devised by pupils when using 'Peer feedback'.
- Self-assessment to be used more frequently.
- Visual prompt posters to be designed by pupils to support teachers and pupils in giving and receiving feedback.

At the end of the school year, the research methods used to collect evidence will need to be repeated and compared to the original findings. SLT can then consider if the new practices to our marking and feedback systems have had an impact on pupils' progress and achievement.

From conducting the action research project, it has been clear that although there was some good practice in our school, it was not consistent. Because of this, the impact on learning is not evident from the work in pupils' books or from discussions with them. Although I initially wanted to measure the impact on learning through the pupils' end-of-year assessments, I realised that this would not be possible as it would have to be done over a much longer period and after the recommendations from this research have been implemented.

With regard to data, on average all pupils are expected to make six sub-steps' progress in a year. Although some of the pupils with SEND I selected had made this progress, it was not evident that marking and feedback had been instrumental in achieving this. As the ten selected pupils have a range of SEND needs, I would like to find out which feedback method is individually preferred. For example, it is already clear that pupils who were on the autistic spectrum did not like their work being written on, nor did they like reading or responding to written comments. Verbal feedback and marking work with the teacher seemed to be their preferred style and it is something that will be monitored over the next year.

I have found that there are many characteristics of effective feedback, but Chappuis (2015) states there are five she considers to be effective, all of which were identified within my findings and we need to make sure we do these consistently:

1   Effective feedback directs attention to the intended learning, pointing out strengths and offering specific information to guide improvement.

2   Effective feedback occurs during the learning, while there is still time to act upon it.

3   Effective feedback addresses partial understanding.

4   Effective feedback does not do the thinking for the student.

5   Effective feedback limits corrective information to an amount the student can act upon.

It is apparent that although the focus of this research was aimed at improving the learning of pupils with SEND, I feel that the outcomes can and will benefit the whole school in fostering continuous growth and development through high quality feedback and marking. Quality feedback and marking is among the most critical influences on pupil learning and now is the time for our school to get it right and provide the most appropriate ways for all our pupils to progress and succeed. We need to make sure that pupils can answer the three major questions identified by Hattie et al. (2016) to ensure that our feedback is effective, whether written or verbal: Where am I going? How am I going? Where to next? In addition, as a staff team, we must also consider – is it motivating, meaningful and manageable?

Recommendations for reading

DfES (2017) *More Impact, Less Marking Toolkit*, London: DfES

This is a useful toolkit written by teachers showing a wide range of approaches to marking and feedback whilst reflecting on the benefits and drawbacks to the pupils' learning. It includes checklists used, pupils' work and, more importantly, pupils' views.

Education Endowment Foundation (2016) *A Marked Improvement? A Review of the Evidence on Written Marking*, London: Education Endowment Foundation.

This shares the views of teachers and the research findings of seven useful areas of written marking. Each section provides information about a wide range of marking strategies and the impact they may have in classrooms and on pupils' work.

Hattie, J., Masters, D. and Birch, K. (2016) *Visible Learning into Action*, Abingdon: Routledge

This is an interesting read of case studies undertaken in countries all over the world looking at 'visible learning', which is the concept of seeing clearly what teachers are teaching and what learners are learning. The case studies show the varying approaches used and the impact these had on pupils.

Houghton, A. (2014) *Engaging Teaching Assistants in Marking and Feedback*. Available online at: www.loynelearningalliance.co.uk/Projects. This article considers the findings from a research project undertaken with teaching assistants and would be easy to adapt to use in your own school. It is thought provoking as it questions how teaching assistants feel about giving marking and feedback to pupils and what the current practice may be in your own school. The article has some useful ideas for future developments.

References

BERA (2018) *Ethical Guidelines for Educational Research*, London: British Educational Research Association

Chappuis, J. (2015) *Seven Strategies of Assessment for Learning*, 2nd edn, New York: Pearson Education

DfES (2004) *Excellence and Enjoyment: Learning and Teaching in the Primary Years*, London: DfES

DfES (2016) *Independent Teacher Workload Report Group. Eliminating unnecessary workload around marking*, London: DfES

EEF (2016) *A Marked Improvement? A Review of the Evidence on Written Marking*, London: Education Endowment Foundation

Hattie, J., and Timperley, H. (2007). The power of feedback. *Review of Educational Research*, 77(1): 81–112

Hattie, J., Masters, D. and Birch, K. (2016) *Visible Learning into Action*, Abingdon: Routledge

NASEN (2018) SENCo/ALNCo Guidance for School Inspection: School improvement for SEND. Available online at: www.nasen.org.uk (Accessed 18/06/19)

Wilson, A. (2012) Student engagement and the role of feedback in learning. *Journal of Pedagogic Development*, 2(1). Centre for Learning Excellence: University of Bedfordshire.

Chapter 4

Increasing the effectiveness of teaching assistant support

Laura Inglis

Context

My school is a larger than average-size infant school and the proportion of pupils who have special educational needs and/or disabilities (SEND) is twice the national average. It is situated in a third-generation mining village that is classed as an area of social deprivation. On roll we currently have 310 children, with 65 of these on the SEND register. This all brings its own set of unique challenges and rewards. The majority of our children have speech, language and communication needs (SLCN) and/or social, emotional and mental health (SEMH) needs. The Educational Psychologist who works with us considers these needs to result from environmental factors, especially within the children's formative years.

Due to our high number of children with SEND, I have been successful in securing funding for 14 children. Within school we have 16 teaching assistants (TAs), with ten of these exclusively supporting children with SEND. While planning my research project, these TAs worked in the following ways:

- 1:1 support with individual children to assist progress towards their IEP targets and those set by the Support Service for Special Educational Needs (SSSEN). This often involved the TA sitting beside a child to break down tasks and repeat learning where needed.
- Supporting children with SEMH and SLCN needs in a Nurture Group in Foundation Stage. This was at the ratio of two staff to six children.
- Undertaking interventions set by individual class teachers, within classes.

For the purpose of this project I wanted to investigate whether our current use of TAs to support individual children predominately through

1:1 support was the most effect practice we could offer. I was concerned that if a child is over-reliant on working 1:1 with an adult as a partner, are we limiting their ability to learn from their peers?

Research such as that of Sharples et al. in *Making Best Use of Teaching Assistants* (2015), has shown that 1:1 TA support may have little or no impact on a child's learning, whereas working with a child in small group settings has a more beneficial result. This is echoed by the *Teaching and Learning Toolkit* (EEF 2018), which identified that, on average, peer tutoring added five months onto a child's learning and TA support added one month, especially where this substituted, rather than supplemented, teachers' teaching. Mindful of this, I decided to first research staff attitudes towards current TA support, use this to plan and implement necessary changes, and then evaluate the impact of this.

While speaking to children informally prior to this project, some commented that always having an adult supporting them made them feel different from their peers and sometimes they just wanted "to have a go by myself". In *Keys to Inclusion*, Wilson and Newton (2011) discuss relationships with TAs, arguing that these can have a negative impact on learning when:

- additional adults provide too much 'suffocating' support and create dependence
- peers are prevented from becoming involved in supporting individuals and modelling areas like communication and learning.

I felt at the beginning of this project that this all reflects where our school is not being as effective with TAs as it could be, limiting the progress of some of our learners with SEND.

Strategy

I started by carrying out research to establish a baseline of school practice and staff attitudes towards our current effectiveness of TA support. I thought this was crucial because prior informal discussions indicated that class teachers had very different views on this to the TAs: teachers believed that it was the TA's job to only work with 'their' child and to be within a class to help with the behaviour management of some of the more challenging children. In contrast, during a staff meeting, one TA questioned why TAs were dealing with behaviour instead of the school trying to find root causes. This reflects the published view of an older student:

Many students who display "challenging behaviour" or find themselves in trouble at school behave this way because they are unhappy in school. As much as this is no excuse to misbehave, if schools paid any interest in their students and their needs I believe that they would not show "challenging behaviour" and misbehave (Anon 2014: 10).

At our school I do believe that we show interest in our children's needs, but sometimes we rely on TAs to cater for these needs as a reaction to their behaviour, rather than asking what is making them unhappy.

I then analysed my baseline research to identify where key changes were required and implemented these over one full term, before measuring the impact and reporting on my findings.

Collecting evidence to measure impact

Evidence collection

For my baseline research I used the following methods:

- Questionnaires to four SEND TAs (based in Key Stage 1). These were handed out in a staff meeting and a box was provided for their return to keep responses confidential. Within these questionnaires, I asked their views on what was working well, what could be improved, current interventions and their effectiveness, and any improvements that could be made.
- A meeting with our Senior Management Team (SMT) to discover their views on what was working well with our TAs and provision, and what they felt could be improved (the SMT comprises three senior teachers – one from each of FS2, Year 1 and Year 2). I asked them questions based on those given to the TAs as I wanted to be able to compare their responses to see if expectations were similar or different. I decided to use this sample of teachers rather than all teachers due to the demands and constraints experienced by teachers at this time of year.
- Analysis of notes from a planning meeting with the headteacher for the next academic year, where current provision was discussed.
- A selection of four target children who are currently in receipt of funding were tracked in the following ways:

  a   academic results at two key assessment points in June and December
  b   through 'pupil voice' – comparing their views in June with December, after changes have been implemented.

Throughout this research project I ensured that my ethical approach had integrity, following BERA guidelines (2018). I avoided any harm for participants and all were assured of confidentiality and anonymity. Participants were made aware of the purpose of the project and that their views would be used to inform future practice in school. All staff gave their verbal consent for their views and evidence to be used within the research project and the public domain. The children were asked for their consent, as was the consent of their parents.

My main findings from the baseline research identified there was a belief that if a TA was allocated to a child with funding, then they should only be supporting that child. The main method of this support was through 1:1 support, as highlighted in my classroom observations (completed prior to this project in my role as SENCO as part of a school improvement observation schedule) and the view of one TA, who described in her questionnaire, a strength of the school was that: "TAs have time to work on children's individual targets as well as SSSEN set tasks and class activities which would not normally be possible without a 1:1 TA." This belief echoed comments made within the SMT meeting: "It means the children get an adult's time to work on tasks that we would struggle to do without that support, such as IEP work and stuff." However, other TAs said that: "TAs should be used for intervention groups, boosters etc. not just general class support" and they "struggle to get time to take children to do interventions". They also raised the importance of matching staff skills to different interventions: "Due to Key Stage time constraints and lack of overall time management, skilled professionals who have knowledge of 'Makaton', for example, may work in Year 1 but a child in Foundation Stage 2 might have benefitted from support."

These quotes were revealing about the time restraints that teachers face in trying to deliver a very packed curriculum in addition to catering for the individual needs of learners with SEND. This was apparent from one of my SENCO observations where I saw that a child who is on the SEND register, but has yet to secure funding, was being disruptive within a classroom. When I spoke to him and asked how I could help, it became apparent that he did not understand the task and all three adults within the room were busy helping other learners. I am certainly not suggesting that this child was just being ignored, but it was evident that the funded children in the class had two adults supporting them, while he was not receiving needed support. After the session, I asked the teacher how learners without funding were supported and was told, "Well, it is really tricky as I try to get to them as often as I can, but there are many children like Child A; I know I should be doing more. If they could get funding then that would help."

Since becoming SENCO, I have managed to secure a large amount of funding for children and associated TAs; however, my research has highlighted a growing issue within school. Staff felt that if a child was on the SEND register then automatically I should be applying for funding as that child needed 1:1 support, rather than consider larger-scale interventions such as Nurture, Positive Play, TalkBoost, and Numicon that could be used to target more learners. The reliance was mainly on 1:1 support throughout the day, which TAs saw as their main job role. This failed to recognise the many other skills TAs have and their training for different interventions; none of these were mentioned.

Interventions were seen very much as add-ons, completed as and when they were needed, and were often pushed to one side when other demands arose, which did not provide any consistency. When asked for evidence to show what impact current interventions were having, it was evident that few assessments were being carried out to measure this. Intervention groups were not seen as a vital tool for ensuring the progress of learners, or to provide essential opportunities for children to learn from their peers and imitate positive learning and behaviours.

Research from academics such as Sharples et al. (2015) identifies that TAs delivering targeted interventions in one-to-one or small group settings consistently show an impact on pupils' progress for approximately three to four months' progress, but crucially:

> these positive effects are only observed when TAs are used in structured settings with high quality support and training. When TAs are deployed in more informal, unsupported instructional roles, they can impact negatively on pupils' learning outcomes (Sharples et al 2015: 23).

My concern was that due to the informal and unsupported role TAs were playing in school, we could be having a detrimental effect on our children's learning.

Children's views also echoed the ethos within school that TAs were there to work 'just with them'. Although I believe that the TAs and class teachers were doing this with the best intentions, it wasn't always what the children wanted, as Child A stated: "I want to work on my table more with the red group." This child often works on a table just with a TA, but clearly wanted to work more with a class group. While the children's views highlighted plenty of good practice and a genuine respect towards the staff, a reoccurring theme was that they wanted to play and learn alongside their friends. This was demonstrated by Child C who described how much she was upset that her medicine regime was completed during playtimes, which meant she missed out on playing with her friends.

Although this was not affecting her academic progress, it was having an effect on her emotional well-being, so we agreed we would trial changing her medicine times and measure the impact this had.

Further data evidence showed that although the target children made some progress between May and July, this was not accelerated progress (see Table 4.1 below showing the children's progress in 'p' levels for those working in Key Stage 1 or 2, but not yet at National Curriculum levels or using the Early Years Foundation Stage scores, including the Early Learning Goals – ELG).

Children in Foundation Stage are assessed using the Early Years Curriculum which is split into age group bands described in months (e.g. 40–60, 30–50, 22–36) and then the Early Learning Goal (ELG). Within each band a child is judged to be beginning (B), secure (S) or developing (D). For children in Key Stage 1 or above who have SEND, 'p' levels 1–8 can be used to assess progress – with P1 being the lowest and P8, the highest (These are now being phased out and replaced by 'Scales of engagement'.) The Leuven Scale is used to assess a child's well-being and involvement. The scale starts at point 1 – where a child shows very low involvement and will often be upset and disengaged – to point 5, where a child is happy, relaxed and fully involved with his/her learning.

After analysing all of my baseline research findings, I created a summary and reported this to my headteacher:

- 1:1 support was appropriate in some situations, but not always the most appropriate solution for learners with SEND to progress (EEF 2018), so learners with SEND should be provided with many opportunities to interact and learn alongside their peers.

Table 4.1 **Progress in P levels**

Child	Reading		Writing		Maths		Leuven scale	
	May	*Ju ly*	*May*	*July*	*May*	*July*	*May*	*July*
A	P6	P6	P5	P6	P6	P7	3	3
B	Y1 B	Y1 S	Y1 B	Y1 S	Y1 B	Y1 S	2	3
C	ELG(B)	ELG(S)	ELG(B)	ELG(S)	ELG(B)	ELG(S)	2	2/3
D	30–50 months (B)	30 –50 months (D)	30–50 months (B)	30–50 months (D)	22–36 months (S)	30–50 months (B)	2	3

- The belief of staff that children with funding automatically require 1:1 support needs to be addressed, as often the child would benefit from support in many different ways such as paired work with peers and small group work. The Deployment and Impact of Support Staff in Schools (DISS, 2009) study identified that TAs were most effective when working 1:1 or in small groups with children using specific interventions for which they were trained, as opposed to more informal general support: one of its key recommendations was 'that pupils in most need should get more, not less of a teacher's time' (Blatchford et al. 2009: 10). This conflicts with our current practice within school, where children were being supported 1:1 by a TA within class or spending large portions of the day out of the classroom with a TA, so are accessing less of the teacher's time.
- Interventions were inconsistently applied across key stages and within classes. These were not given priority and measurement of their impact was not analysed or reported. Research shows that children respond better in a group with peer role models: 'Children learn from each other by copying. Let us give them a great range of role models to help them develop communication, learning and social skills' (Wilson and Newton 2011: 48). Interventions are a good opportunity to facilitate this whilst having an impact on other learners, not just those with funding.

I then suggested the following model:

- Children to be supported within class on a 1:1 basis as needed, but incorporated into their table groups wherever possible, with work made accessible and achievable by the class teacher using IEP targets as necessary.
- In the afternoon, TAs would be assigned intervention groups to run with six children from each year group. Suggested interventions included:
  a   TalkBoost
  b   Numicon
  c   Gross Motor Skills
  d   Positive Play
  e   Nurture.

It was agreed that this model would be rolled out for the next academic year and would have an interim review in December to measure impact.

Impact

In December, I repeated the research methods used to measure the original baseline. I used the same questionnaires and questions, as I wanted to be able to directly compare results. I also analysed academic progress for the children in addition to measuring the impact of each individual intervention.

A full timetable of afternoon interventions had been implemented throughout Key Stage 1 during the Autumn term and TAs' work with their target children in the classroom for the mornings shifted in focus from 1:1 work to small group work wherever appropriate. This had an impact on individual learners, who were happier with the opportunities to learn alongside their peers: "Me is a big boy now. I smiling as I work with my friends. My friends help when it's tricksy. Mrs Y also helps sometimes" (Child A). This was also reflected in comments made by the SMT regarding support within class in the mornings: "It helps to have the TA working with a group rather than just 1:1 as it means more children are helped and encourages the child with funding to be more independent. They seem to enjoy working alongside their friends mor." (Teacher A). Child C also showed that she was much happier now she got to "play out" alongside her peers at break-times, with her Leuven score moving up from 2 to 4.

The five different interventions were all conducted in different areas of the school. This was agreed so that TAs were less likely to be distracted or required to deal with behaviour issues in classes. It was decided that a baseline would be established for the interventions at the beginning of every term and assessed at the end of each term, with the impact measured and reported to the SENCO. In the period from September to December, 22 different children benefitted from attending interventions groups, including 16 from the SEND register and six with funding. This shows that other children without funding and not necessarily on the SEND register also benefited from interventions and provided crucial peer models for their peers.

Academically, the children made good progress within the intervention groups, although one child had significant social issues at this time (see Table 4.2 below).

TA questionnaires showed that interventions were proving successful and offered opportunities to work with a wider range of children, giving their target children more independence, with one commenting: "Both these interventions groups seem to be working well and I have noticed an improvement, especially in TalkBoost." They did however, sometimes note that interventions were "rushed and they would like more time to complete these" – which is an action point that needs to be addressed going forward.

Table 4.2 Progress within intervention groups

Child	Reading		Writing		Maths		Leuven Scale	
	Oct	Dec	Oct	Dec	Oct	Dec	Oct	Dec
A	P6	P8	P6	P7	P7	P8	3	4
B	Y1 S	Y2 D	Y1 S	Y2 B	Y1 B	Y2 B	3	4
C	ELG(S)	Y1(B)	ELG(S)	Y1(B)	ELG(S)	Y1(B)	2	4
D	30–50 months (D)	40–60 months (D)	30–50 months (D)	40–60 months (D)	30–50 months (S)	40–60 months (B)	3	4

Overall, the whole the ethos within school has shifted from considering funding to be purely for 1:1 support to looking at what provision we can make through interventions and 'quality first teaching'. This has made our applications for funding easier, as I can now clearly demonstrate what we were currently providing. Daily struggles still exist in changing some more experienced members of staff's attitudes that children with SEND should have 1:1 support, and if they have SEMH and behavioural issues they should be removed from the classroom because they are disrupting others; but on the whole, most staff are more positive about this new approach and understand the theory behind it.

Through a discussion at my 'Coffee and Chat' Session, (a termly group I set up to give parents and carers of children with SEND an opportunity to talk to one another, as well as to me) parents reported that their children enjoy the interventions and working with friends. Some confusion still remained around children with funding having their 'own TA', so careful explanation was needed to clarify why this was not always the most appropriate form of support and that group or paired work has been shown by research to be more effective.

In conclusion, the intervention timetable and organisation of TAs has been proved to be more effective and have a greater impact on children's learning since the completion of this action research project. Gradually, staff attitudes are changing towards accepting different methods of support and academic progress is improving due to targeted interventions with TAs matched to their skill sets. Most importantly, children are happier with the arrangements offering them targeted support and their own independence. These conclusions were recognised in our most recent Ofsted report which stated:

> The special educational needs coordinator has a very good understanding of her role. She knows each pupil and their background

well and is determined to improve the outcomes for pupils who have special educational needs and/or disabilities. Consequently, the vast majority of these pupils make good progress from their starting points and the additional funding provided for them is used well.

Recommendations

Recommendations for practice

1 Hold discussions with your senior management team about the benefits for children of working within small groups or within the classroom. It needs to be a whole school approach to move away from the culture of children having 1:1 support and this can only happen if your senior management team are on board!
2 Be prepared for some initial negativity as people are often resistant to change, but if you ensure that you record a baseline for all interventions and regularly assess progress, you can show everybody the impact of interventions.
3 Talk to children who have SEND – by taking their views into account you will often find that they don't want to be out of the classroom or always have an adult glued to their side. They want to be included with their peers.

Recommendations for reading

Wilson, D and Newton, C. (2011) *Keys to Inclusion*, Nottingham: Inclusive Solutions Publications
  This was really useful reading – it opened my eyes to different approaches for including learners with SEND.

References

Anon (2014) 'A matter of respect', *Inclusion Now*, 39:10. Online, available at: https://issuu.com/chloeatallfie/docs/inc_now_39. (Accessed 14/12/18)
British Educational Research Association (BERA) (2018) *Ethical Guidelines for Educational Research*, London: BERA
Blatchford, P., Bassett, P., Brown, P., Martin, C., Russell, A. and Webster, R. (2009) *Deployment and Impact of Support Staff in Schools*, London: Department for Children, Schools and Families
Sharples, J., Webster, R. and Blatchford, P. (2015) *Making the Best Use of Teaching Assistants*, London: The Education Endowment Foundation

EEF (2018) The Teaching and Learning Toolkit. Available online at: https://educationendowmentfoundation.org.uk/uploads/pdf/Teaching and Learning Toolkit. (Accessed 30/12/2018)

Wilson, D. and Newton, C. (2011) *Keys to Inclusion*, Nottingham: Inclusive Solutions Publications.

Chapter 5

Becoming SEN champions

Amy Breeze

Context

This research took place at a sixth form college in the Midlands. It has approximately 500 pupils on roll who come from a variety of feeder schools. Students have to complete an application form and there are entry requirements to secure a place. Initial communications of support needs are recorded at the application stage. The last OFSTED inspection (2015) rated the provision as outstanding. Most students are white British and the proportion of disadvantaged students eligible for support through pupil premium funding is well below the national average. As a college, the proportion of students who have a disability or are considered to have Special Educational Needs (SEN) is also below the national average.

Over the last few years, legislation and practices that have governed the delivery of provision for young people with SEN have developed understanding and increased expectations. In 2004, the Government's 'Removing Barriers to Achievement' strategy emphasised that all teachers must expect to teach students with special educational needs and that schools should look to an inclusive approach as part of their ethos and school culture. The momentum and focus that this initiative gathered has ensured that school leaders, SENCOs and teacher training programmes have embedded professional development to ensure that schools 'meet the needs of pupils rather than expecting them to fit in, reflecting current discourses on the social model of disability' (Richards 2010: 109).

This current climate of accountability has resulted in training sessions and programmes that can often be received with pessimism by staff because they focus on skill development auditable against a 'higher' agenda – for example, attaining targets set in a school development plan or meeting OFSTED criteria – rather than developing an enhanced understanding of pedagogy. One of the main barriers to implementing provision for students with SEN continues to be teachers' attitudes (Avramidis et al. 2000; UNESCO 2014; Saloviita 2018), but this is often not addressed. Government policy and teacher education providers' response to meeting these 'auditable skills' affects decision-making on course priorities for teacher training, resulting in programmes that concentrate on topics like planning and curriculum, rather than reflection on personal values and beliefs which could benefit their inclusive classroom practice (UNESCO 2014).

As a teacher at my college and beginning the SENCo role, it had become apparent that there was a gap in knowledge and some assumptions about provision for students with SEN that needed resolving. This reflects Rieser's earlier view (2013: 12) that:

> Teachers feel ill prepared and often unwilling to make the changes necessary to include them [people with physical and/or mental impairments]. Governments add to these problems with inaccessible buildings, rigid curricula, assessments and failure to provide sufficient inclusive teaching materials and support.

I began building an 'SEN vision' for the college, working with my colleagues whose own pedagogy came with varying levels of confidence in providing provision for the students in their classrooms with SEN. Previous research I had carried out into student and parent voice at the college had shown me that students with SEN and their families can find education systems extremely frustrating, with one parent exclaiming:

> I would love the question to be asked: are his needs being met? Is he kicking off because someone doesn't understand or he is fed up in the lesson because he can't make progress?

Strategy

After speaking about my concerns to the Senior Leadership Team in my SEN Link Meetings, it was agreed that a Continual Professional Development (CPD) training session would be beneficial in reaffirming classroom practice for students with SEN and to explain reform changes. I needed to build a training session that would, according to Desimone (Finefter-Rosenbluh 2016: 2), provide a 'framework of activities that seek to enhance teachers' knowledge and skills, which may also contribute to their personal, social, and emotional growth'. At the same time I was aware of the need to overcome some barriers that may prevent our teachers from engaging with new training material, such as their own teaching styles, curriculum restraints, their current knowledge and experience, and preference for style of training delivery.

The *Special Educational Needs and Disability Code of Practice: 0–25 Years* (DfE 2015: 62) clearly states that alongside the Local Offer:

> Securing expertise among teachers, lecturers or other professionals to support children and young people with SEN or disabilities – should include professional development to secure expertise at different levels: awareness, enhanced and specialist.

Reviewing the definitions given in this Code, it became apparent that I needed to plan an enhanced level of training that would give advice on teaching and learning for those working with young people with SEN on a regular basis. I wanted staff to feel more confident in their own approaches to improve attitudes towards differentiation and inclusion, while ensuring that the training was age and college appropriate.

As part of my planning, I returned to the concept of the SENCO as a strategic leader where the emphasis was on improving provision rather than merely maintaining practice. Strategic leadership 'entails anticipating change or events, envisioning possibilities, maintaining flexibility and empowering others to create strategic change as necessary' (Cheminais 2015: 31). I was particularly drawn to the idea of 'empowering others'; this not only suited the graduated approach of SEN provision (Code of Practice 2015), which placed teachers as the initial contact in the team around the child, but was also a positive, affirming concept that placed confidence in individuals, rather than relying on an 'expert' role model.

Drennon and Foucar-Szocki's belief (Diaz-Maggioli 2004: 24) that 'as individuals learn, so does the entire group. Authority shifts from outside experts to practitioners inside the program who come to develop and articulate theories grounded in their real-world experience', resonated with me. So, I decided that if I could empower our teachers to take control of, and share, their practice, SEN provision would strengthen as part of the college ethos and improve staff confidence in making inclusive practice within all subject areas. Aligning with this concept, I was introduced to a TED Talk from Rita Pierson (2013) in which she encourages educators that 'every child needs a champion'. These 'champions' would be activists in making their college inclusive and support not just the child, but the team around the child to safeguard positive outcomes. This inspired me to create the focus for my CPD session: 'Empowering Champions of SEN'.

Collecting evidence to measure impact

Evidence collection

Before I could begin planning my CPD session, I needed to establish a baseline of knowledge among all staff at the college to compare this with results after the training. I created a simple descriptive survey (Lankshear and Knobel 2004), designed to identify the characteristics of a sample at one point in time. I used the online software SurveyMonkey and chose this platform because it allowed me to email the survey directly to everyone – I anticipated that it would be seen and returned by the highest percentage of staff, as most preferred to complete surveys electronically. Questions covered SEN policy content and relevance, responsibility for SEN, understanding of key terms and a how confident staff felt about SEN provision. The final question asked teachers to identify what they would like for further training.

I placed a deadline on returning the survey to make sure I could analyse the results prior to planning the CPD, so I could shape the session around staff's level of knowledge. Although I was aware that this training would be aimed at teaching staff primarily, I felt it was important to secure the views of all staff at a baseline level to instil that the whole school community has a role in inclusion. All staff were invited to the training.

In order to comply with the British Educational Research Association's *Ethical Guidance for Educational Research* (2018), I took the necessary steps to ensure that all participants who took part in the survey and the training session understood why I was undertaking the research and how it would be used and reported on, so that I could gain their voluntary informed consent. Staff were also given the right to withdraw from taking part in the survey and research activities associated with the training. I also sought the approval for the use of quotations, sound bites and documentation to be used within the session and ensured that anonymity was maintained throughout; this included permission to use an old EHC plan as an example of this documentation.

Impact

Prior knowledge (the baseline)

The staff survey delivered some interesting results that helped me structure the focus of my training session: 48 out of 70 staff returned the survey; 16 respondents felt that the SEN policy in practice was evident in the college, though 15 others responded that they 'didn't know'; 28 staff were unaware of where the SEN policy was and of its contents; and 47 felt that it was most relevant to teaching staff. There were also some varying assumptions on SEN definitions: 22 staff recognised that the subject teacher was responsible for the progress of students with SEN, but only 25 staff felt 'fairly confident' in differentiating their lessons to include students with SEN – a number that I hoped to improve as a result of the training session.

Once I had my baseline, I was able to shape my training session around the results. I was allocated a 2-hour session in the summer term. In order to 'empower champions' I was keen that the session would include activities that placed the emphasis on staff reviewing their own practices or raising questions about policy, adopting Cheminais' view (2015: 85) that 'teamwork, as a cooperative and collaborative process, empowers others to develop professionally, with each person bringing a range of knowledge, skills and expertise'. The concept of Quality First Teaching (QTF) was then a driving force behind the main body of the session to reinforce that teachers must use their best endeavours to include all needs within their classrooms. I also used Diaz-Maggioli's guidance (2004) on what good teacher centred professional development training should involve. Figure 5.1 explores how I developed this guidance and addressed it in my training session.

The session

I set out the room by moving the tables into four clusters to suit the four areas of SEN outlined in the Code of Practice (*Cognition and Learning, Sensory and Physical, Communication and Interaction, Social, Emotional, Mental Health*) that would correspond to group work later in the session. The session ran with the following structure:

1 **Survey results.** As staff entered, a slideshow displayed the pre-training survey results.
2 **Voice.** Staff listened to snippets from interviews with parents and students with SEN to share how the system could let these families down.
3 **Picture starter.** Each table was given four pictures to discuss how they related to the history of SEN provision.
4 **History.** I gave a history of legislative practice, reform and the 2015 Code of Practice.
5 **EHC plan.** I explained changes from 'statements' to EHC plans. Staff then looked at an EHC plan example.

Purposeful and articulated	Participatory and collaborative	Knowledge based	On-going	Developmental	Analytical and reflective
Purpose stems from the school community	Participants work together and participate in the learning process	Both the wisdom of practice that resides in the school and more conventional research	It is to respond to shifting contexts	Both participants and the staff development process	Calls out attention to the importance of knowing one's path

Sourced from Diaz-Maggioli (2004: 22)

Purposeful and articulated	Participatory and collaborative	Knowledge based	On-going	Developmental	Analytical and reflective
MY OBJECTIVE: Use existing knowledge of staff to structure training session and strengthen inclusion in the college	MY OBJECTIVE: To share good practice and inspire good practice through teamwork and collaboration: putting the teacher as director of provision	MY OBJECTIVE: To use current policy/ practice and teachers' experiential learning alongside research on leadership and legislation	MY OBJECTIVE: To make staff aware of the implications of the 2015 Code of Practice	MY OBJECTIVE: To EMPOWER staff to feel confident in planning and delivery inclusive provision across the college and strengthen the inclusive ethos of the college	MY OBJECTIVE: To EMPOWER staff to be self aware of what it feels like to be an outstanding practitioner and to reflect on their own current practice and how they might improve it

Figure 5.1 How guidance was developed and addressed

6 **College policy.** Staff were reminded where to find and what important documents were relating to college provision, such as the Information Report, SEN Policy and links to the Local Offer. They were informed of where they would find the 'Register of Need' in college and given outlines of key staff responsibilities.

7 **Group definitions.** Each table created their definition of SEN and read these out. I then gave the Code of Practice definitions.

8 **Person around the child and Waves Model** (DFES, 2006). Explanations, personalised for the college, focused on the importance of QFT. I then further defined QFT.

9 **The Inclusive Classroom.** Discussion of what makes a classroom inclusive supported by work carried out by Inclusive Solutions, which I experienced as part of my SENCo qualification.

10 **Think/Say/Do/Feel task.** Staff filled in sticky notes on a grid responding to the question: What would you expect people to think/say/do/feel of an SEN Champion?

11 **Empowering good practice.** Each table created a mind map based on an SEN category assigned to their table about what QFT was already happening at the college.

12 **Autism and dyslexia training.** The baseline survey identified these two areas had the greatest interest for more information.

13 **Case studies.** Each table looked at a few case studies written specifically for the college, discussed and then feedback how they would support those prospective students (see Figure 5.2).

14 **Being a champion.** The session finished with Rita Pierson's 2013 TED Talk: *'Every Kid needs a Champion'.*

| Joe sent in an application to the college on which he signposted that he has dyslexia. Joe achieves straight C grades for his GCSEs. Joe has chosen to study three academic subjects and one creative subject. Joe's folder is collected from his feeder school and his previous school acknowledges poor handwriting, slow processing speeds and that Joe struggles to copy down from the board. He also had Access Arrangements for his GCSE exams. | Omar sends in an application to the college and signposts that he has an EHC Plan for his Autism and OCD. His feeder school and external agencies have worked hard with Omar to establish some strong coping mechanisms for his OCD. Omar is a bright student and hopes to go on to study French at university. Omar has to line up his things on his desk and gets upset when they are disturbed. He has issues with cleanliness and proximity and if he gets upset-he will count numbers in his head to huge quantities. He likes red foods. | Emily sent in an application to the college on which she signposted that she is a wheelchair user. Emily achieves a range of grades for her GCSEs including some high scores. Emily has chosen to study four academic subjects: one of which is Biology. Emily uses an electronic wheelchair. She has fine motor skill issues and some self-esteem issues. |

Figure 5.2 Three case studies for discussion

Feedback and evaluation

At the end of the training session I asked staff to complete a Post-Training Survey to measure opinions and progress against the baseline survey. Due to staff availability on the day, out of the 17 teachers that took part (including the headteacher and assistant principal), all felt confident in differentiating their lessons, a large improvement from the baseline survey. All 17 participants now fully acknowledged the responsibility of the subject teacher for the provision of students with SEN and also rated the SEN policy as evident in every aspect or some aspects of the school community. To support any staff who could not attend, I created a condensed version of the activities and offered it two weeks later at the end of the day, while also ensuring all notes were available on the college intranet for reference.

Staff responded well to the session. They participated in all activities and asked some interesting questions. It was clear that everyone had similar but varied definitions of what special educational needs were, but the concepts they discussed led them to see that umbrella terms encompass a wider range of issues. Activities that were aimed at empowering them as 'SEN Champions' worked well, especially when they shared inclusive practice and contemplated individually how it would feel to be recognised as a 'champion'. Staff found the 'Think/Say/Do/Feel' activity a little awkward at first, but once they had placed a few sticky notes, discussion opened up about how it would instil confidence in a person to be recognised with these traits.

By including parent and student voices in the session, I was able to share why I was a passionate advocate about ensuring that these students felt secure, safe and included both within the classroom and as part of our college community. Some staff fed back that they were shocked at the inconsistency of care and differentiation; such reactions avowed for me that an achievement of the session would come in the self-reflections of practice to ensure they were 'champions' in their classrooms. The session was described as "really brilliant" and another colleague said that I "inspire confidence", which was humbling and reinforced that there were already several aspiring 'champions' in the college.

It was a couple of months after the training that one of the parents whom I had interviewed previously wrote me an email saying: "It is refreshing to see words translated into action after a lifetime of just words!" This confirmed that there had been an impact from the session and new 'champions' existed amongst the staff.

Recommendations

Recommendations for practice

The discrepancy in survey numbers (48 base survey/17 post-training) makes the statistical evidence a little harder to quantify. A possible disadvantage of using a simple descriptive survey is that limited answers may not allow 'every shade of response' (Lankshear and Knobel 2004: 167). It is difficult to measure whether a person is genuinely feeling 'empowered' to always be aware of their responsibility for young people with SEN and make inclusive provision. I felt that I had achieved the outcome to instil confidence in the staff due to the positive output from the session, both verbally and through the survey result. However, to expand on this research for a deeper insight into the confidence of staff and their teaching and learning practice, a longitudinal study could be carried out that involved completion of a survey at the start and finish of an academic year, supported through observations and staff interviews (possibly as part of the performance management process).

Timing allowed for the session was important. I did run out of time during the session by approximately 15 minutes. This particularly had an impact on the amount of time we were able to spend looking at the case studies; these in particular had been created as college specific studies, so it would have been beneficial to have spent more time analysing how staff would respond to those examples. It wasn't necessary perhaps to have the starting activity and the slides on SEN reform, but I felt this painted a picture alongside the testimonies that it was an area of professionalism where major changes had occurred and so it was important to acknowledge the expectations of these on our practice.

Themes that arose during the training session required opportunity for reflection. For example, there seemed to be a correlation between what is considered as Quality First Teaching and what OFSTED deems to be the criteria of an outstanding lesson. If a school already has an outstanding rating then it could be perceived as automatically providing Quality First Teaching for students with SEN. This could have both negative and positive effects on the confidence of teaching staff: to be an outstanding practitioner could also instil confidence in your ability to differentiate in an inclusive classroom, or it could lead to assumptions about practice. In the session it was clear that leadership staff were able to reflect on teaching and learning practice already seen at the college, allowing them to instantly appraise the college's success. This does, however, reflect earlier concerns about accountability and skill sets being auditable against a 'higher' agenda that draws away from the original objective and aims of the training.

What I felt was key were the benefits of me delivering in-house training for colleagues, rather than using an outside provider. Being able to make distinct comments and use examples that relate to our professional environment was paramount in gaining the understanding of the teachers who participated. Although it was necessary and informative to spend some time looking at the implications of SEN policy reforms, I feel that empowering staff to be aware of their own strengths, skills and pedagogy, and to share collaboratively with others, developed individual teaching and learning – and this made the project successful.

It was unfortunate that only 17 attended the training. Potentially, this had an impact on whole-school practice in championing SEN. I would recommend that to foster a culture of inclusion, training be scheduled and made compulsory for all staff or, as a minimum, a lead representative of all staff teams attends, so that training can be further disseminated in all departments. Additionally, all new members of staff must be trained on SEN provision. I would recommend that the concept of 'SEN Champions' should be built upon within school communities – to also teach students about the brilliance of difference and how they might become a champion too – and that this concept could go beyond SEN into other social, moral aspects of the school ethos.

Recommendations for reading

TED Talks Education (2013) Every Kid Needs a Champion.

Rita Pierson's compelling talk is a must if you feel inspired to become a 'champion' too.

Diaz-Maggioli, G. (2004) Teacher Centered Professional Development, Virginia: ASCD

If designing your own CPD or encouraging the sharing of good practice, this text may reinforce your ideas.

Richards, G. (2010) 'I was confident about teaching but SEN scared me': preparing new teachers for including pupils with special educational needs, Support for Learning, 25(3): 108–115

This acknowledges the important of SEN awareness with new teachers.

References

Avramidis, E., Bayliss, P. and Burden, R. (2000) Student teachers' attitudes towards the inclusion of children with special educational needs in the ordinary school, *Teaching and Teacher Education*, 6: 277–293

British Educational Research Association (2018) *Ethical Guidelines for Educational Research*, London: BERA

Cheminais, R. (2015) *Handbook for SENCOs*, 2nd edn, London: Sage

DFES (2006) *Leading on Intervention*, London: DFES

Diaz-Maggioli, G. (2004) *Teacher Centered Professional Development*, Virginia: ASCD

Finefter-Rosenbluh, I. (2016) Behind the scenes of reflective practice in professional development: A glance into the ethical predicaments of secondary school teachers, *Teaching and Teacher Education*, 60: 1–11

Department for Education/Department for Health (2015) *Special Educational Needs and Disability Code of Practice: 0 to 25 Years*. Available online at: www.gov.uk/government/uploads/system/uploads/attachment_data/file/398815/SEND_Code_of_Practice_January_2015.pdf (Accessed 01/17/19)

Lankshear, C. and Knobel, M. (2004) *A Handbook for Teacher Research*, Maidenhead: Open University Press

Pierson, R. (2013) *Every Kid Needs a Champion*. TED Talks Education. Available online at: www.ted.com/talks/rita_pierson_every_kid_needs_a_champion (Accessed 01/17/19)

Richards, G. (2010) 'I was confident about teaching but SEN scared me': preparing new teachers for including pupils with special educational needs, *Support for Learning*, 25(3): 108–115

Rieser, R. (2013) Educating Teachers for Disabled Children: UNICEF Project. *Inclusion Now* 35: para.56

Saloviita, T. (2018) How common are inclusive educational practices among Finnish teachers?, *International Journal of Inclusive Education*, 22(5): 560–575

UNESCO (2014) *A Guide for Ensuring Inclusion and Equity in Education*, Paris: UNESCO

How does a daily run affect the concentration, attention and behaviour of children, especially those with ADHD and/or behavioural difficulties?

Lara Krause

Context

The school in which this small-scale research study took place was a larger than average-sized city primary school. The majority of pupils are from a white British background and the proportion of children with a disability or special educational needs is above average. There are 35 children on the SEND (special educational needs and disabilities) register and these children have a range of difficulties that include autism, Down syndrome, dyslexia and attention deficit hyperactivity disorder (ADHD).

My action research investigated the effect that a daily run has on children with ADHD and/or behavioural difficulties. This was selected because although our latest OFSTED report stated that the behaviour of pupils in school was 'good', there were children with behavioural difficulties and/or ADHD who could affect the learning environment for themselves and others. Six of these children took part in the study from across three classes, to see if a daily run would have a positive effect on the learning environment for both them as individuals and their classes.

Strategy

I decided to trial a daily run for this research because I was inspired by the Daily Mile initiative (2016) in which pupils from some schools in Scotland ran a mile each day. The Daily Mile website (2016) highlights the many benefits that this running initiates, including the improved emotional state, concentration and behaviour of pupils. I discussed the idea with a Behaviour Support Worker from our local education authority, who recommending trialling this physical activity so that I could see if the benefits worked for our pupils and positively affected their learning.

The daily exercise involved a 10-minute run around the school grounds with a member of staff supervising. The children ran every day for three weeks so there was a measurable period. Three whole classes were involved in the study: a Year 1 class (27 children) and two Year 3 classes (21 and 22 children). These were chosen because they had a larger proportion of children identified with ADHD and/or behavioural difficulties within them. All of the children in the Year 1 class ran for 10 minutes every morning, whereas those in the two Year 3 classes ran twice (in the morning and again in the middle of the afternoon), as our junior children do not have an afternoon playtime like the Year 1 infant class.

The selected group

Six children were selected for my research study, two in each of the three classes. They either had a diagnosis of ADHD or regularly displayed challenging and disruptive behaviours in the classroom.

Attention Deficit Hyperactivity Disorder is a psychiatric disorder which affects 5% of school age children worldwide (Bussalb et al. 2019). The National Health Service (NHS 2016) describes people with ADHD as having symptoms of 'behavioural problems' that could be categorised into 'inattentiveness' and 'hyperactivity and impulsiveness'. The use of the word 'problem' reflects, in my view, a perspective of the medical model of disability in which difficulties are seen to solely lie within individuals and an ethos of providing disabled people with methods to 'normalise' their lives (Holloway 2004). In contrast, the social model of disability suggests that society creates disabling barriers for an individual, which lead to social exclusion, so it is these barriers that need to be removed, rather than an individual being 'normalised' (Clarke 2006).

As a Special Educational Needs Coordinator (SENCO), I aim to support the view of the social model and seek to use these ideologies within my practice. As there is a correlation between academic underperformance and ADHD (Bussing et al. 2012) and children with ADHD experiencing difficulties in controlling their behaviour (ADHD Foundation 2016), I wanted to use this research to discover if a daily run could improve the learning environment experience for children with ADHD and therefore increase their potential for learning and help self-managed behaviour.

Collecting evidence to measure impact

Evidence collection

A range of research methods was used to collect data for this study, including questionnaires, recording of behaviour, a memory task and a handwriting task, which all 70 children completed. These were used for baseline assessments during the first three weeks of the six-week research period when the children did not undertake any running and then repeated after three weeks of the daily run activity; this allowed for data to be compared between times before the children were running and after the trial had been completed.

Our school uses a 'warning' behavioural system. Children may receive warnings if they display negative behaviours and break the school rules. These warnings were recorded throughout the research period for all children in the three classes so that behavioural incidents could be compared between the times when the daily run was, and was not, taking place.

The NHS (2016) states that people with ADHD often have difficulties with attention, which can cause them to become easily distracted and affect their ability to concentrate on tasks. So, I chose two methods of data collection that could record any differences with attention. The first method was a memory test where all the children had 3 minutes to silently remember 16 words and pictures presented on the board and then had 5 minutes to record as many of them as possible. This was repeated with different words before and after the three-week running activity to compare the results.

The second method involved them copying a piece of the same text for 5 minutes, before and at the end of the research period after their final run. The children had the same text for the baseline and final assessments; however, the Year 1 class had a different text than the Year 3 classes, with shorter words and age-appropriate content. The texts had unusual words so the children were forced to concentrate to spell the words correctly. For this assessment, I considered the amount of words the children copied correctly and the neatness of their handwriting as an indicative measurement of their attention levels.

Questionnaires were used as a qualitative form of data collection because they can provide useful information about the values and attitudes of the respondents (Burton and Bartlett, 2005) and were a time-effective way to gather the views of 70 children on two occasions. I designed a questionnaire to ask the children about attitudes towards their own behaviour and whether they believed that the daily run activity had an effect on them. This enabled the children's opinions to be heard, something I considered important as Singh (2012) suggests that a significant amount of literature about ADHD silences children, and their voices and opinions are rarely heard. The children answered this questionnaire before any running had taken place and after the three weeks' trial. The teachers of the Year 1 and Year 3 classes also completed two short questionnaires, rating all the children's behaviour and concentration before and after the running project.

To ensure the research was ethical, I followed the BERA guidelines (2018): parent consent forms were sent home with a letter explaining the research and I gained informed consent from the children; staff gave their consent to take part; and all participants had the right to withdraw, were kept anonymous and had the research explained clearly to them. Three parents and one child opted out of the research element, so their data were not used (none of these children had ADHD). The study was approved by a university as part of my National Award for SEN Coordination coursework.

Impact

Behaviour warnings

To compare children's behaviour, the number of warnings was recorded during the three weeks before the daily run trial started and for the three weeks when it took place. The results showed (see Table 6.1) that while the daily runs did not prevent children receiving warnings, the number given was reduced. During the three weeks prior to the trial, 406 behaviour warnings were issued – averaging 5.8 warnings per child. During the period of the daily runs, a total of 274 warnings were issued, giving an average of 3.9 warnings over the three-week period – a significant decrease.

The results displayed in Table 6.1 show that children received fewer warnings during the weeks they were participating in daily runs. It is, however, interesting to note that the percentage decrease was slightly more for all the children, rather than those with ADHD and/or behavioural difficulties. The studies of two researchers might be relevant to consider here:

1   Singh (2012) identified that children with ADHD often complained of being 'wound up' by other children. It would be interesting to extend the daily run trial over a longer period of time to see whether the number of warnings for children with ADHD then decreased more because their peers' improved behaviour resulted in less provocation.

Table 6.1. Number of warnings issued

	Total warnings for all children	Total warnings for 6 children with ADHD and/or behavioural difficulties
For the 3 weeks prior to the daily run activity	406	124
For the 3 weeks during the daily run activity	274	87
Change	-132	-37
Decrease	32.5%	29.8%

2   Research by Honkasilta et al. (2016) discovered that young people with ADHD found it difficult to make 'good' behaviour choices when other children around them were making 'bad' behaviour choices, as they often copied them to meet normative behavioural expectations. So, if the majority of children are making more good behaviour choices when participating in a daily run activity, this could lead to children with ADHD making fewer poor behaviour choices and might improve their scores further if the daily runs continued.

Attention and concentration

Analysis of the memory test results indicated that the children's memory improved after they had been running, as they could recall more items from the list of sixteen objects they had to remember. Figure 6.1 shows the combined memory test results of all the children and the increased score of 137 after they had completed the running project.

Figure 6.2 shows the memory test score for the six children with ADHD and/or behavioural difficulties. All six children increased their score after the three-week daily run activity by an average of 3.17, which suggests that a daily run may have helped increase their attention and improved their learning potential. However, more in-depth research would need to be undertaken, with a larger sample and for a longer period, to identify if it had significant effects on children's learning.

When analysing the difference in the children's handwriting, it was evident that there were some changes in the style and neatness of writing for some of the children before and after the three-week running period, as well as the amount of work they produced. However, it seemed that the running activity only made a positive impact for one child (who had a diagnosis of ADHD) from the selected group of children with ADHD and/or behaviour

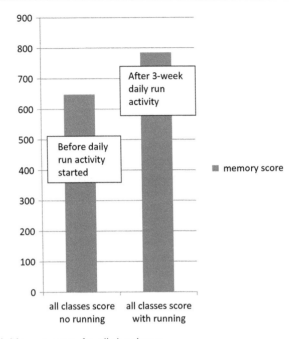

Figure 6.1 Memory score for all the classes

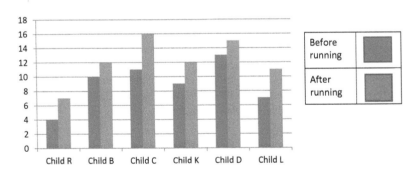

Figure 6.2. Memory test scores for the six children

difficulties. Child D wrote 16 more words in the time given after participating in daily running. Although there were no significant differences for the other children within the group, this might reflect the findings of Strong et al. (2005), whose research indicated that children need to participate in a significantly large amount of sustained exercise to have substantial benefits in their behaviour and concentration.

Questionnaires were given to the children before starting the daily run activity (to establish a baseline) and again after three weeks of daily running. In the first questionnaire, three of the selected children described their behaviour as 'bad', two as 'OK' and one as 'good'. In the second questionnaire, after completing three weeks of running, only one child had this perspective, with the others viewing their behaviour to be 'OK' (3), 'good' (1), or 'very good' (1).

The children also answered questions on whether the daily runs helped their concentration and behaviour. Five out of the six selected children stated that they enjoyed completing the daily runs and believed these had helped their concentration and improved their behaviour: Child D did not enjoy completing the daily runs and did not believe they helped behaviour. These views could suggest that if children enjoy an activity, then they are more likely to perceive it to be having a positive effect on them.

At the end of the questionnaire there was an opportunity for children to write their own opinions of the 'good' and 'bad' things about daily running. Their responses were generally positive, even for Child D:

> You get fresh air, it improves your fitness, it makes my behaviour better. It's all good. (Child K)
> I get out of breath but it gets rid of some of my energy. (Child D)
> It's good I guess, I like racing my friends (Child L)

The questionnaires completed by the three class teachers before and after the daily run trial asked how they rated children's concentration when completing quiet work. All three teachers stated that their concentration had improved after running, classing this as 'good' or 'very good'. Two out of the three teachers also noticed a specific improvement in the concentration of children with ADHD and/or behavioural difficulties in their class. However, having originally described this as 'very poor', they still said it was 'poor' or 'OK'.

At the end of the questionnaire teachers had an opportunity to express their opinions about the daily runs after the three weeks' trial. They gave many positive comments, with one teacher writing:

> The louder children returned calmer and are more able to concentrate … they return to the classroom calmly and ready to learn. Class 3 loved running and plan on continuing to run next year.
>
> It's a quick and fun method to get everyone moving and there does seem to have a positive effect on certain children. The children loved getting outside the classroom every day. It was great to see them settle quickly afterwards.

However, the other Year 3 teacher felt that any positive effects of the run did not last the whole lesson, stating: "There is a short-lived calmness, but no overall long lasting effect." This again could link to Strong et al.'s (2005) research findings, which suggested that a longer period of exercise was needed for a significantly beneficial effect on children's behaviour.

Recommendations

Recommendations for practice

After completing this research there are some recommendations and considerations that I would suggest for other teachers and schools interested in taking part in a daily run.

Introducing the idea of a 'daily run' needs to be school-wide so that all staff are aware of benefits this exercise may have and understand why children are taking time out of their lessons to do this. In our school, even after a short trial, a daily run did appear to have benefits for the whole class, as it reduced behavioural incidents and improved the concentration of the majority of children who took part. It also improved this for children with ADHD and/or behavioural difficulties; however, it cannot be seen as a 'cure', because these children did still have behavioural incidents.

One obstacle that may occur when planning to implement a daily run during the school day is the amount of time it takes, as teachers often feel pressured to fill their day with 'academic' lessons and meet many targets. From my experience, if a daily run is considered as worthwhile by senior leaders in the school, then teachers will feel at ease in initiating this activity. The benefit of the approach I took was that it only lasted 10 minutes and it did not involve children getting changed, so the short time out of lessons to incorporate a run was worth the improvements in concentration and behaviour it brought.

Teachers and other staff in the school need to be aware of the traits of children with ADHD and able to adapt their practice to suit individual's learning styles. I view a daily run as one method that can reduce behavioural incidents for children with ADHD and so reduce situations of their social exclusion in school: even if teachers do not feel comfortable taking part in a run every day they should consider the idea of a 'movement break', especially in the afternoon in KS2 when children may be expected to sit still for a long period of time. This will enable all staff to work towards creating a more ADHD-friendly environment where children have opportunities to release their energy, to work and be included in a calmer classroom.

Reflections on the research

Action research is usually conducted by focusing on a small sample. This research only involved three classes from one school and cannot represent all children, or all schools. Therefore the results from this research only reflect that of the sample used; a much larger sample would need to be used to identify a more reliable view of how a daily run affects children, especially those with ADHD. Also, the results tests were taken immediately after the three-week trial, so they represent the immediate effects from this. To develop this study further, the tests should be repeated after a longer time period to see if these promising results from our daily run trial extend past the short-term positive effects.

Recommendations for reading

The Daily Mile website (www.thedailymile.co.uk) has clear information about the benefits of running and has free resource packs for schools that wish to take part. This may be useful when sharing the idea of a daily run with staff members.

The "Sheriff's Challenge" is an initiative in Nottingham (other schools can take part) to encourage children to run 100 miles (www.nottingham schools.org.uk). It is a light-hearted competition to get the children engaged in running each day and compete against other schools.

References

ADHD Foundation (2016) *What is ADHD?* Available online at: www. adhdfoundation.org.uk. (Accessed 03/06/19)

BERA (2018) *Ethical Guidelines for Educational Research*, London: British Educational Research Association

Burton, D.M. and Bartlett, S. (2005) *Practitioner Research for Teachers*, London: Sage Publications

Bussalb, A., Congedo, M., Barthelemy, Q., Ojedo, D., Acquaviva, E., Delome, R. and Mayard, L. (2019) Clinical and experimental factors influencing the efficacy of neurofeedback in ADHD: A meta-analysis, *Frontiers in Psychiatry*, 35(10)

Bussing, R., Porter, P., Zima, B. T., Mason, D., GarvanC. and Reid, R. (2012), Academic outcome trajectories of students with ADHD: Does exceptional education status matter? *Journal of Emotional and Behavioural Disorders*, 20: 131–143

Clarke, H. (2006) Prevention of Social Exclusion of Disabled Children and their Families: A Literature Review, The University of Birmingham, Research Report, DFES 782, Nottingham: Department for Education and Skills

Holloway, L. (2004) Childhood disability and ability: (Dis)ableist geographies of mainstream primary schools, *Disability Studies Quarterly*, 24(3)

Honkasilta, J., Vehmes, S. and Vehkakosi, T. (2016) Self-pathologizing, self-condemning, self-liberating: Youths' accounts of their ADHD-related behaviour, *Social Science and Medicine*, 150: 248–255

NHS (2016) *Attention Deficit Hyperactivity Disorder (ADHD) – Symptoms.* Available online at: www.nhs.uk/conditions/Attention-deficit-hyperactivity-disorder. (Accessed 03/06/19)

Singh, I. (2012) VOICES study. Final Report, London, UK. Available online at: http://www.adhdvoices.com/documents/VoicesReport2012. (Accessed 03/06/19)

Strong, W., Malina, R., Blimkie, C., Daniels, S., Dishman, R., Gutin, B., Hergenroeder, A., Must, A., Nixon, P., Pivarnik, J., Rowland, T., Trost, S. and Trudeau, F. (2005) Evidence based physical activity for school-age youth, *The Journal of Paediatrics*, 146(6): 732–737

The Daily Mile (2016) *About the Daily Mile / The Daily Mile UK.* Available online at: www.thedailymile.co.uk/getting-started/about/. (Accessed 03/06/19)

Chapter 7

Moving up to 'big school'

Rosemary Brooks

Context

My school is a selective grammar school for boys (with a co-ed sixth form) that has served a small, rural market town in the Midlands for over 400 years. It has been judged to be a good school in the last two Ofsted inspections. There are currently circa 800 students on roll, of which 7.5% have identified learning needs, with two having an EHCP. Our intake is drawn from around 40 primary schools and from two different local authorities. We are quite unique for a selective setting in that we have a bespoke student support suite with a small, but highly experienced team of three non-teaching support staff, and in 2018 the headteacher and governors agreed to the role of SENCO becoming a part-time, non-teaching role.

As Head of Year 7, I had worked to develop an effective transition process but, on becoming SENCO in 2015, a new question posed itself: Are we doing enough to challenge community perceptions regarding SEND provision in a selective setting through our promotion of the school? Are there parents who remain to be convinced that we could meet the needs of their child with SEND? Can our established practice be justified by the existing research into transition from primary to secondary school?

My study, therefore, set out to review the school's current transition process in the light of parent and pupil surveys, available literature about this and others' good practice, to ascertain its efficacy in meeting the needs of students with SEND. It also considered the effectiveness of our promotional materials and activities in giving parents the confidence to choose a selective setting for a child with SEND.

Strategy

I was unable to identify any academic articles uniquely addressing the transition of students with SEND to a selective setting. However, an exploration of pupil and parental preferences in studies on transition did identify some areas for consideration and confirmed that our current practice could reviewed against the evidence from those studies.

Ofsted last reported nationally on primary transition in 2002, but in 2015 they published a report *Key Stage 3: The Wasted Years* which looked at the transition process as part of its review of KS3. Sir Michael Wilshaw, who commissioned the report, commented: 'The importance of a good start to secondary school education cannot be overstated. School leaders need to have a clear understanding of their pupils' achievements in primary school and build on them effectively from the day they start secondary school life' (2015). The report also stated that primary headteachers 'supported the view that pastoral transition for the most vulnerable was an area of strength, with secondary schools providing bespoke arrangements tailored to the needs of individual children' (Ofsted 2015: 18). However, while the importance of supporting social needs and vulnerable students was also highlighted in the recommended Deepings School case study, the report also recommended 'that transition from Key Stage 2 to 3 focuses as much on pupils' academic needs as it does on their pastoral needs' (Ofsted 2015: 18).

Attainment might appear to be perhaps less of an issue in a selective setting. However, the Ofsted report concluded that 'Leaders prioritise the pastoral over the academic needs of pupils during transition from primary school. While this affects all pupils, it *can have a particularly detrimental effect on the progress and engagement of the most able*' (Ofsted 2015: 7). Attainment does come into focus when we compare 11+ outcomes with CATs (Cognitive Abilities Tests) outcomes. There can be some significant anomalies between these two outcomes where students have had intensive coaching for the 11+. Without appropriate support, the risk to the self-esteem and progress of these students is significant. We have also found that teacher assessments could sometimes be skewed by the size and ability range of the pupil sample in their primary school. Our response, even prior to the demise of NC (National Curriculum) Levels, was to devise our own descriptors on the transition forms for identifying attainment levels in Maths and English, in order to establish more reliable baselines in these subjects for our school setting.

Nobody would dispute that an unhappy child will not be a successful learner, but do we really acknowledge how much of a 'sea-change' secondary school is for our students? Mandy et al. (2016) approach transition for children with ASD from a clinical perspective, but their summary of the challenge secondary school represents makes very clear the level of this Year 7s face: 'The transition from primary to secondary education ... is a major ecological shift that poses considerable social, emotional, academic and organisational challenges' (2016: 5).

Coffey (2013: 268) points out that it is not just a sea-change for students, but also for their parents:

> Parents too are forging relationships with the new school. ... Rather than enjoying reasonably ready access to their child's teacher, they now have to forge relationships with a number of teachers. At the same time their children are beginning to seek independence and no longer wish to be seen in the company of their parents.

We therefore place considerable value on pre-transition meetings as an opportunity for students to make their wishes known and encourage parents to allow their son or daughter to drive support planning.

Our decision that transition is overseen by the Head of Year 7, enabling a more cohesive approach to the whole transition process and establishing a positive home-school relationship with parents as they face letting their child move into greater independence, reflects Coffey's recommendations. This approach also recognises that transition is an even greater concern for parents of children with SEND, who understandably worry about how their child will cope with the additional challenges they face.

Collecting evidence to measure impact

Evidence collection

There are two key strands to our transition process. The first is Year 5 Taster Days held in June each year and hosted by Year 8 students. These are open to any pupil considering an application to our school so that they can get a taste of the pace and level of work in a selective setting and a feel for our ethos. After considering the research guidance of Burton and Bartlett (2005), I decided that an online survey using SurveyMonkey to be the most effective way of ascertaining the views of prospective students and parents – who at that point had no formal connection to school – regarding our transition process and website information. This would be more quantitative in nature and caution needed to be exercised in drawing conclusions from individual opinions, but it could also be effectively compared with existing data gathered from historic feedback forms completed on previous days.

The second and main strand is the Year 6 transition process. This starts with a visit by a member of the pastoral team to meet the pupil in their primary school, followed by an induction evening in July to meet the form tutor and fellow classmates, and then a full induction day at the end of that week. The SENCO also invites parents and students with SEND to meet her during the induction evening to ensure that preliminary plans are appropriate. We have a staggered start in September with Years 8–11 starting back a day later than Year 7. This allows the Year 7 students a day to orientate themselves in a less crowded environment and enables us to provide bespoke induction activities for them. We hold a settling-in review for parents with the form tutor in October to enable early intervention for any who are struggling to settle. The SENCO also attends this review afternoon so any preliminary plans for students with SEND can be reviewed. There is also a Year 7 'Parents' Information Evening' in September that explains our tracking and support systems.

Due to other commitments when this research project took place, interviews with individual students with SEND proved the most manageable means of capturing student views. Parent views were already available from our established process linked to the settling-in reviews, so data collected over several years allowed an identification of trends. This approach also enabled me to probe the different perceptions of need on a more qualitative basis. For my student interviews I opted for prompts on key aspects rather than set questions, so that I could adjust wording to suit different students.

In accordance with BERA guidance on ethics (BERA 2018), consideration was given to the question of informed consent and the right to withdraw. Interviews with students were therefore, optional and took place in an informal context during downtime on the school's Sports Day. These focused on their own personal experience of transition, but were also designed to give students an opportunity to suggest how we could improve the promotion of the school to new students. Consideration was also given to the students' capacity to consent. In our setting, students are routinely involved in the school's self-evaluation process and were therefore deemed to have sufficient capacity to be fully aware of what they were consenting to. Students were asked to give consent *before* they took part and were completely free to opt out. I was confident that students would be honest about their wish to take part, but was also clear that should any show any signs of discomfort I would terminate the interview. Students whose comments were used would only be identified by their Year group and learning need.

Prospective parents and students were invited to complete the online survey via a letter addressed to parents that the Year 5 and 6 pupils took home. It outlined the purpose and scope of the survey, and encouraged pupils to complete the survey as well as their parents. The survey also included a question relating to consent and all responses were anonymised.

The school has always sought the views of new parents and students as part of our transition process at the Year 7 'Information Evening' in September and then prior to the 'Settling-In Parent-Tutor' meetings held in October. The second consultation has proved the most useful in terms of assessing the effectiveness of our transition practice and allowed for a review of trends over six years.

Impact

Student interviews

The interviews with our own students proved to be very informative. Indeed, their suggestions of possible ways to improve transition support were included in the Year 5 and 6 surveys with a view to testing their appeal. Their review of current processes confirmed that the support they receive from the Student Support Team has had a significant impact on their transfer to secondary school which was clearly valued. A Year 10 student with Asperger's Syndrome summed up the support he had received since Year 7 as: "Massive. I'd still be the near bi-polar emotional wreck I was in Year 7." Another Year 8 student with autism stated: "They helped with problems and not knowing what to do ... problems with other people. I knew where to find them if I needed them." The individual emotional support they receive was also valued as another Year 8 with autism described: "[They] helped me to be less angry. Seeing Mrs W each morning has helped." The role of the wider staff team was also commented on favourably by a Year 7 student with autism: "Most of the teachers were really nice. Dr R said things from his own life that helped get to know him."

One of the most valuable contributions they made to this study was to identify ways we could improve the promotion of the school's support for transition in general as well as for students with SEND on the school website: evidence of "People working hard and enjoying themselves"; "Examples of Year 7 work and end of Year 7 stuff" to address the perceptions of work being "too hard"; "People's opinions on the school – highlights of the term from Year 7" to showcase the support they receive; and information about "the learning support people and the number of people they've helped".

Online surveys

The two Year 5 Taster Days in June usually attract up to 250 pupils with a range of abilities. However, while the completed surveys confirmed that our processes were popular with both Year 5 and Year 6 parents, the number of responses was very low and only contained two responses from parents of children with SEND and only one Year 6 pupil response. This was disappointing, but led me to revisit the question as to whether some parents did not see their child with SEND as being compatible with a selective setting and so had not applied for a place on the Taster Day. Nevertheless, the small sample did confirm the common concerns that parents and pupils have: Year 6 respondents identified academic demand, homework, organisation and coping with travel while Year 5 respondents further identified getting lost and coping with lots of different teachers and older students. The surveys also confirmed the value of many core elements of our transition programme, with the highest ratings being given to primary school visits, meeting tutor and form mates on the 'New Intake Evening' and having a specialist team of Year 7 tutors. The proposal of a dedicated transition section on the school website received support from 70% of Year 5 respondents.

Induction data from previous years

A review of the induction data from the last six years confirmed that the key concerns for parents and students are, in the main, the same each year. For students with SEND these concerns will be shared, but undoubtedly some may be exacerbated by their learning difficulty or disability. The summary table below (Table 7.1) shows the nature of the key transition concerns for pupils and their parents. Table 7.2 summarises which of the core elements of our current programme were found to be most helpful.

Table 7.1 identifies that the prevailing concerns for Year 7s and their parents are mainly the social and practical demands of any secondary school, although the academic demands in a selective setting may be of concern to some. Table 7.2 confirms the value of our various transition activities.

Transition processes

The review of the current processes and protocols with a specific focus on students with SEND did highlight some areas for improvement. As admission to the school requires pupils to have passed the 11+ test, it is critical for a school claiming to be inclusive that this first step towards becoming a student is accessible to pupils with SEND. The 11+ registration form now includes a section specific to learning needs to ensure that we are able to offer reasonable adjustments during the admission process.

Table 7.1 Transition concerns for new pupils and parents

Data obtained from: Year 7 parent surveys pre/post-transition and Year 5 and Year 6 parent/pupil surveys

	Pre-transition	Post-transition	Year 5 survey	Year 6 survey
Nature of concerns (in rank order of concern)	Getting lost in big school	Organisation	Finding way	Level of work
	Homework	Homework	Level of work	Organisation
	New friends	Issues with work	Different teachers	Homework
	Difficulty of work	Travel	Organisation	Travel
	Travel to school	Friendships	Homework	Finding way
		No concerns	Travel	Older boys

Table 7.2 Transition activities considered to be most helpful

Data obtained from: Parent 'Settling-in' survey and Years 5 and 6 parent/pupil surveys

Settling-in survey	Year 5 surveys	Year 6 surveys
Taster Day	Primary visits	New intake evening in July
Sports opportunities	Meeting tutor in advance	New intake day in July
Tutor/Tutorial time	Discrete Year 7 tutor team	Staggered start (Year 7 Day 1)
Staff support	Information evening in September	Mix of induction and lessons on Day 1
Social activities	Homework life per subject	Information evening in September
Nominating a form friend	Help getting to bus-stop on Day 1	Induction pack
	Induction pack	Settling-in reviews in October
	Settling-in reviews in October	Meeting tutor in advance
		Visit to primary school

A selection of transition forms available online were reviewed and their content informed the production of new primary school transition forms. We revised our general primary school transition form to ensure both pastoral and academic needs are identified, and introduced a specific SEND transition form designed to provide us with a clear picture of support in the feeder school to inform our support planning. These transition forms can be completed and submitted electronically by primary school staff, making the processing of information much quicker.

We have also now established pre-transition meetings with parents, pupils and primary support staff to ensure that our 'Personal Education Profile' details effective support and reflects the wishes of individual students, in keeping with the 2015 Code of Practice. The benefit of additional induction days was identified, and these are now part of our enhanced transition package. Prospective parents attending open days are encouraged to book a meeting with the SENCO prior to registering for the 11+, to explore how we can best meet their child's needs. The SENCO and student support team also attend Parent Consultation Evenings to be available to discuss any emerging needs.

While we appear to support our students with SEND effectively, the question remains as to whether there are barriers for prospective students that we are still not addressing. We are arguably unlikely to have had contact with parents who automatically dismissed our school as an option because we are selective, but we perhaps need to accept that they might exist. A project on the Alliance for Inclusive Education (ALLFIE) website exploring historic transition experiences around secondary education (*How Was School?*) revealed that many disabled children were simply denied access to a grammar school place either due to physical barriers or a simple misplaced assumption that they would not cope with the academic demands. I would hope that attitudes have changed for children today, but in the face of increasing claims of inadequate provision for pupils with SEND we cannot be complacent.

Recommendations

Recommendations for practice

Tutor–Parent 'Settling-In Reviews' in October are in line with Coffey's view that 'having some form of parent/teacher event early in the first term in the new school can be important in avoiding situations where a lack of awareness of procedures can lead to misunderstandings' (2013: 268). Topping's research supports a staggered start: 'Close the school to all students except new entrants, even if only for the first day' (2011: 281). He also emphasises the importance of being aware of the significant changes Year 7s face as they get to grips with the socio-emotional realities of life at secondary school: 'Transition is often accompanied by a decline in self-esteem and motivation, involving changes in identity and the construction of self' (2011: 280).

Byrne (2013) identifies that a key requisite for parents of a child with SEND is for her/him to be seen as an individual person, rather than a child with a label of need. He references the research of Bagley and Woods (1998) who identified that 'the dominant value perspective for parents of children with SEN is the intrinsic-personal/social and the choice of school is therefore oriented around the child as a person' (Byrne 2013: 130). My research does suggest we can be confident that our processes support this. However, how do we connect with parents whose perceptions of a selective school may be founded on misconceptions and a belief that their child will not cope with the demands of the work because of their additional needs? Ultimately, we need to be engaging with local parent/carer forums and giving parents the opportunity to explore if a selective setting could be a viable option for their son or daughter. Clearly, for children with significant or severe cognitive impairment, the 11+ may prove insurmountable, but there are children with SEND who have the intellectual capacity for a selective education but need reassurance that their social and emotional or physical needs can be accommodated.

Mandy et al. (2016: 6) focus on the challenge faced by students with ASD, one of the largest groups of need presenting at our school:

> [S]econdary schools demand greater academic and social indepen-dence from their students. Thus, the transition ... involves a major ecological shift, which makes a number of demands on a child's social, intellectual and organisational capacities...

However, these challenges are not unique to students with SEND, so a cohesive and inclusive approach to transition for *all* students has to be at the heart of good inclusive practice.

Recommendations for reading

How Was School? ALLFIE website: howwasschool.allfie.org.uk/.

This gives personal accounts of past educational experience that should inspire a greater drive for inclusion.

Coffey, A. (2013) Relationships: The key to successful transition from primary to secondary school? *Improving Schools,* 16: 261–271; and Topping, K. (2011) Primary–secondary transition: Differences between teachers' and children's perceptions in Improving Schools, *Improving Schools,* 14(3): 268–285

These papers by Coffey and Topping focus on the personal challenges around transition that should be shaping our processes.

References

BERA (2018) *Ethical Guidelines for Educational Research*, London: BERA

Burton, D. andBartlett, S. (2005) *Practitioner Research for Teachers*, London: Paul Chapman Publishing

Byrne, A. (2013) What factors influence the decisions of parents of children with special educational needs when choosing a secondary educational provision for their child at change of phase from primary to secondary education? A review of the literature. *Journal of Research in Special Educational Needs*, 13(2): 129–141

Coffey, A. (2013) Relationships: The key to successful transition from primary to secondary school? *Improving Schools*, 16: 261–271

Mandy, W., Munn, M. and Baykaner, O. (2016) The transition from primary to secondary school in mainstream education for children with autism spectrum disorder, *Autism*, 20: 5–13

Ofsted (2015) *Key Stage 3: The Wasted Years*, Manchester: Ofsted

Topping, K. (2011) Primary–secondary transition: Differences between teachers' and children's perceptions in Improving Schools, *Improving Schools*, 14(3): 268–285

Wilshaw, M. (2015) *Too Many Students Let Down in Early Stages of Secondary School*, Ofsted Press Release (10/09/15)

Chapter 8

The impact of introducing 'key adults' to support children with challenging behaviour

Jill Turner

Context

This study was based in a South of England primary school with 220 children from Nursery to Year 6 on the roll. The school is situated in an area of significant deprivation – the deprivation index was 0.38 compared to a national average of 0.24, with 60.1% of children qualifying for free school meals (compared to a national average of 26.6%).

My action research study was set up following a period of significant change within the school that included two teachers leaving mid-year and the headteacher of nine years announcing in December she would be leaving at the end of the summer term. This had created an air of instability within our whole school community and the amount of unacceptable behaviour in school increased. This resulted in a rise in exclusions, with a small number of children receiving several fixed-term exclusions.

To try to stabilise behaviour across the school, a specialist behaviour class was started. This was led by a teacher who had previously worked in pupil referral units and for the Behaviour Support Service, a Higher Level Teaching Assistant (HLTA) and two other teaching assistants (TAs) – giving a staff to child ratio of approximately 1:2. The class had eight KS1 children in the morning and seven KS2 children in the afternoon (the children were with their normal class for the other half of the day); all of these children were on the SEN register for Social, Emotional and Mental Health (SEMH) needs that were affecting their academic progress and had had at least one fixed-term exclusion in the previous term. This class was designed as a short-term measure and we were looking at ways to successfully reintegrate them back into their normal class full time. The plan was to reintegrate the children when they were ready and not after a set time, but we hoped that this would be within half a term. We wanted the time out of class to be as short as possible, because we agreed with the Special Educational Needs and Disabilities (SEND) Code of Practice (DfE 2015) view that teachers are responsible for the progress of children in their class even if they are being taught by TAs or other staff. We were also mindful of Higgins et al.'s work in *The Teaching and Learning Toolkit* (2014), where they showed that if the TA was substituting rather than supplementing the children's teaching, then academic progress was compromised.

Some of the children were managing their behaviour and learning by spending half a day with this small group and half a day in class, but others found this more difficult. The focus of my research was to find out whether allocating a key adult to some of the children within this small class would help them return to their normal class successfully and limit further fixed-term exclusions. Demanet and Van Houtte (2012) noted that positive relationships and a feeling of belonging at school helped prevent misconduct, so we hoped that helping these children to form a bond with a key adult and returning to their normal class with this support would decrease inappropriate behaviours and raise achievement.

Several of the children who were placed within this small class had diagnoses of attachment disorders and others showed behaviours which, knowing their personal history, may have also been due to attachment difficulties. We asked our Educational Psychologist (EP) to work with the school and she gave our TAs some training on attachment disorders. This then fed into the introduction of key adults for this small group of children.

Strategy

This research study was dependent upon members of staff working closely with individual children, so I needed to ensure that sufficient adults understood the role and were prepared to be key adults for some of these children. As we have a small staff team in school (fewer than 30), I was able to design and use a semi-structured questionnaire which was printed, put in the staff room and also sent by email (to be printed and returned anonymously). Following ethical guidelines (BERA 2018) a covering letter was included with the questionnaire so that people knew what the questionnaire was for, that completing it was not compulsory, it would be anonymous, and the anticipated benefits of completing the action research project.

This questionnaire explained what a key adult was and included questions on:

- who they thought should be key adults (including whether it should be someone in the child's class or someone in a different class)
- whether they would like to be a key adult or not, and why
- who they thought should be involved pairing up children and adults (i.e. child/teacher/SLT/someone else)
- what problems they thought the role could cause
- how much time it was reasonable for the role to take each day.

The response rate was 55% (15/27) with only three people being unwilling to become a key adult. I decided that this made a small-scale research project viable. Of the returned forms:

- 80% (12/15) indicated that they thought the key adult should be someone in class with the child
- two people responded "Maybe" to being a key adult dependent upon who the child was and whether they knew them well enough to offer support
- 98% (14/15) felt that the children should have some say in who their key adult could be
- predicted problems included what would happen if the adult was out of school and an overdependence on the adult
- everyone felt that the role should take less than 45 minutes a day.

The staff in the specialist behaviour class carried out continuous, detailed observations of: 1) behaviours; 2) interactions between children and children; and 3) interactions between children and adults. This qualitative data was collected by the teacher in his class; although the intention was that he was just an observer, due to the nature of the children and the situations that arose, there were times when he had to become an 'observer-as-participant' (Cohen et al. 2017).

This observational data was originally collected so that we could look at triggers, reactions and behaviour of the children in order to work out strategies that would enable us to help them return to their classes safely. It also provided us with an opportunity to look at children and adult interactions to see if any relationships could be developed into a key adult role. Observations showed that some adults seemed to be able to diffuse difficult situations more easily with different children; there was often no discernible reason, but the ability to be able to calm or distract a child quickly was one we wanted to try to develop.

Following advice from the EP, observations specifically looking at different types of attachment were made using observation checklists (Golding et al. 2013). These were then analysed with her to see if we could establish types of attachment difficulties for the children, as her previous observations of this group had identified that a cause of their behavioural difficulties was linked with attachment issues.

After two weeks, we analysed all of the data and chose three children from KS1 (Child A, Child B and Child C) for whom we thought having a key adult would be beneficial and help them return successfully to full-time class attendance. I spoke individually to the selected children about the role of a key adult, using language at a level they could understand. I told them that we would like to offer them the support of a key adult and explained what they could do to help them – for example, meeting them every morning, listening to them, supporting them talking to other members of staff (Golding et al. 2013).

As I viewed this relationship with a key adult was going to be pivotal to the project's success, the children were told that they would help us choose which key adult would work with them. This was particularly important as children who have attachment difficulties frequently demonstrate a need to feel in control of situations. Having taken the children's opinions and our observations into account, pairings were made. I then approached selected adults to discuss their participation and what it would entail. After I had spoken with key adults, a conversation was then held between the child, key adult and myself to re-explain the role and how we thought it would work and what we hoped it would achieve.

With all of the children chosen for the project, a regular routine of contact was introduced and established before the child was totally reintegrated into their class. All of the adults met 'their' child as they arrived at school to complete a non-threatening, regular task (e.g. engaging with modelling dough or colouring), while discussing with the child what they had done the previous evening and that morning. One key adult volunteered to come into school and meet her child during the breakfast club he attended.

Two children (Child A and Child B) had key adults (Mrs A and Mrs B) who were the TAs based in their normal class (but were not assigned as a 1:1 with them). The key adults were able to speak to their allocated child regularly throughout the day, including planned chats around break time and after lunch. One child (Child C), had a key adult (Mr C) not based in his class, so they planned to meet quickly at break time and then have a chat at lunchtime – which often included them eating lunch together in the hall. When this key adult knew that he was not going to be available at break, he left a blank face on a sticky note in an arranged place for Child C to add an appropriate expression to show how he felt his previous session in class had gone. This helped, as he knew he was still 'being heard' and that Mr C would then discuss the contents of the note with him at the soonest available time.

There was no set end date planned for the use of the key adults as we planned to review their effectiveness weekly after the children returned to class. The intervention seemed naturally and gently to draw itself to a close without having a formal ending, as the children became settled and no longer needed regular support. The relationship between the children and adults remained, and was used in a less formal manner as needed, throughout the rest of the year.

Collecting evidence to measure impact

Evidence collection

Before allocating key adults to any children, Boxall profiles (Bennathen and Boxall 1998) and Goodman's (1997) one page 'Strengths and Difficulties Questionnaires' (SDQ) were completed. These gave a quantitative baseline against which we could measure changes in both behaviours and emotional responses in the class – such as how often they had tantrums, how often they completed tasks or how they considered other children's feelings. The same profiles and questionnaires were repeated after four weeks of working with a key adult. Although the extensive qualitative data enabled us to make hypotheses, adjust things on a short-term basis and then compare overall (subjective) observations, the quantitative data enabled us to have a more objective and direct comparison with some specific characteristics and difficulties identified.

We met weekly with the key adults to discuss how they felt children were progressing and identify if any changes to the intervention were needed. Once the children were back in their class full-time, we interviewed them to find their opinions of having a key adult.

Impact

The introduction of a key adult was seen as a positive strategy by all three children, the key adults and their normal class teachers. All of the children returned successfully to class and over the following term their incidences of unacceptable behaviour were reduced – during the previous term they had received six exclusions between them (totalling seven and a half days) and during the term that they had key adult support, and the following term, they only received one half day exclusion between them.

After four weeks, the SDQ and Boxall forms were repeated by the same adults and all three children showed improvements using this data. Most noticeable improvements for all of the children were in the 'Reduction of Overall Stress' in the SDQ questionnaires and 'Insecure Sense of Self' and 'Negative Towards Others' strands on the Boxall profiles.

Once the children were settled back in class, approximately four weeks after the introduction of the key adult, they were given semi-structured interviews to find their perspective on this support. They were asked:

- Can you tell me what it was like before 'X' became your key adult?
- What does 'X' do to help you?
- Could anyone else help you in class?
- What helps you stay in the classroom to do your work?
- Tell me about 'X'?

All of the children recognised that the key adults were instrumental in helping them and contact at the start of the day was viewed as particularly important. This time of contact was able to be continued by all of the key adults, even when other areas of being a key adult were found to be more difficult or had tapered off.

Child A:

> [*Before Mrs A*] I could do what I wanted. No one would chase me. I didn't have to do my learning. You had to keep phoning A and T (*carers*), they didn't like that! I sometimes got sended home and now I am in class.

When talking about Mrs A and what she did, Child A explained:

> She follows me. She meets me in the morning at the door and we do Lego and talk. She stops me being too naughty sometimes. She looks out for me. I can talk to her – sometimes I have to talk to her, sometimes if I was silly. She is getting good at Lego, I'm showing her how to. She comes to breakfast club with me a bit now. She does Lego at breakfast club but she's not as good as me. I will help her and she can help me.

Child B:

> [*Before Mrs B*] It was uncomfortable. I had no friends, no one would play with me. When I got Mrs B, then they would play with me. She helps me behave. I like it when I tell her my problems – that makes me feel happy. It's better in class with Mrs B. I couldn't be in class without Mrs B.

The trusting relationship was also important, as Child B explained:

> I really like her and she likes me. She still likes me; even if I'm not nice to her she still likes me. That makes me happy.

Child C had an adult who had been the teacher in the specialist class and he recognised that his key adult was sometimes unavailable (this was partly due to different KS1 and KS2 breaks and lunchtimes):

> Well it is good in the morning and he sees me and sometimes he sees me in the day, but not so much now. He did see me and talk to me and take me out to run round and things, but now he is busy with them other kids, but he still tries and see me nearly every day and every morning.

Child C appreciated being 'held in mind' and the plan they had made for when Mr C knew that he would not be available:

> He sometimes leaves me smiley Post-its without faces and I can go up on my own and fill them in at breaks, so he knows what sort of morning I have.

Child C was keen to say how he felt about his key adult:

> He's good. He's cool, he does fast running and I can keep up, sometimes I can run faster, I'm really fast. If he sees me out [of class] when I should be in he talks to me and helps me go in, but sometimes I run out back again. He talks about stuff in the morning and he lets me run around the playground. He comes and sits next to me at lunchtime as well. He eats his lunch with me before running club. He is happy when I say I have got stickers.

This study was limited as we were only able to have three children in KS1 allocated key adults. We would have liked to have been able to see the impact of introducing key adults to some of the KS2 children too to see if the impact was as great. Children were returned full-time to their class following discussions with SLT, staff in the specialist class and the key adults. We did not choose to use a formal reintegration readiness test such as the ones suggested by Doyle (2001), but if we were to repeat having a specialist class with more children, then we would also incorporate this scale to support our discussions around reintegration.

Recommendations

Recommendations for practice

Key adults: The strategy was most effective when the key adult was easily available to the child, but the adult did not need to be a 1:1 for the child. Availability seemed to be very important, so having a key adult in the class seemed to make him/her more effective. Due to the nature of teaching, using a TA who could quickly make contact, even if this was non-verbal contact, seemed to make the role more effective. Having a key adult in class also meant that s/he acted as a bridge whenever the child arrived there – whether this was from the specialist class, an intervention or following him/her absconding. Key adults always made sure that children returning to class were welcomed, regardless of why they had left it.

Choice: Involving children in the choosing of the adults seemed to make the children more engaged with the project. None of the children 'took advantage' of having a key adult, but all seemed more engaged in class, having someone there or knowing that they would be talked to about their time in class.

Time: The most important time for the children and key adult to meet seemed to be in the morning, as soon as s/he arrived at school. If the adult was not available during the rest of the day, just knowing that they were 'held in mind' seemed sufficient.

Recommendations for reading

Geddes, H. (2006) *Attachment in the Classroom*, London: Worth Publishing

This book looks at the principles of attachment theory and why it can cause children to present with different types of challenging behaviour. It is an easy-to-read book that has lots of personal school-based examples and practical ideas for interventions.

Golding, K.S., Fain, J., Frost, A., Mills, C., Worrall, H., Roberts, N., Durrant, E. and Templeton, S. (2013) *Observing Children with Attachment Difficulties in School. A Tool for Identifying and Supporting Emotional and Social Difficulties in Children Aged 5–11*, London: Jessica Kingsley Publishers

This is a book of tools rather than a theoretical read; it is filled with photocopiable observation sheets, checklists and diagrams to help identify emotional and behavioural problems. It helps differentiate between the different types of attachment difficulties, and has hand-outs and activities to provide emotional support and to identify appropriate interventions.

Bergin, C. and Bergin, D. (2009) Attachment in the classroom, *Education Psychology Review*, 21: 141–170

This paper explains what attachment isn't, as well as the different types of attachment and why attachment is important in classrooms.

References

Bennathan, M. and Boxall, M. (1998) *The Boxall Profile Handbook for Teachers*, London: London Nurture Group Network

British Educational Research Association (BERA) (2018) *Ethical Guidelines for Educational Research*, London: BERA

Cohen, L., Manion, L. and Morrison, K. (2017) *Research Methods in Education*, Abingdon: Routledge

Demanet, J. and Van Houtte, M. (2012) School belonging and school misconduct: The differing role of teacher and peer attachment, *Journal of Youth and Adolescence*, 41(4): 499–514

DFE (2015) *Special Educational Needs and Disability Code of Practice: 0–25 Years*, London: DfE

Doyle, R. (2001) Focus on practice: Using a readiness scale for reintegrating pupils with social, emotional and behavioural difficulties from a Nurture Group into their mainstream classroom – a pilot study, *British Journal of Special Education*, 28(3): 126–132

Golding, K.S., Fain, J., Frost, A., Mills, C., Worrall, H., Roberts, N., Durrant, E. and Templeton, S. (2013) *Observing Children with Attachment Difficulties in School. A Tool for Identifying and Supporting Emotional and Social Difficulties in Children Aged 5–11*, London: Jessica Kingsley Publishers

Goodman, R. (1997) The Strengths and Difficulties questionnaire: A research note, *Journal of Child Psychology and Psychiatry*, 38(5): 581–586

Higgins, S., Katsipataki, M., Kokotsaki, D., Coleman, R., Major, L.E. and Coe, R. (2014) *The Sutton Trust – Education Endowment Foundation Teaching and Learning Toolkit*, London: Education Endowment Foundation

Improving the school's universal provision in accordance with changes outlined in the new special educational needs and disability code of practice

Clare Bedford

Context

A key principle of the new Code of Practice is that all children with special educational needs (SEN) should have access to high quality universal provision which meets their needs and ensures opportunities to engage in activities alongside their peers (DfE 2015). Universal provision sets out the basic expectations relating to effective inclusive practice which should be in place to ensure that a setting is prepared for children with additional needs and supports staff to meet the needs of all children (Devon Graduated Response Tool 2017).

The action research reported in this chapter was prompted by an evaluative study undertaken in the school where I work as the Special Educational Needs and Disabilities Co-ordinator (SENDCO). It is a small, rural village primary school currently comprising 159 pupils ranging from 4–11 years old. Our school is part of an Academy chain that includes 12 other schools of varying sizes in south-west England. The school has a higher than national percentage of children with SEN, which is increasing year-on-year. In the past we have supported the needs of SEN-designated children through a statutory assessment, whereas now the children are supported through a range of effective interventions, including Thrive-Online and the Early Help Assessment.

Action research involves the careful monitoring of planned change in practice. It is a cyclical, reflective and collaborative process (Waters-Adams 2006). My research study was designed to initially review and then assess progress towards universal provision. The main objective was to establish whether our classrooms were equipped to cater for the needs of SEN-designated children and how we increase the quality of whole-class provision.

Strategy

In the action research study cycle I adopted, I first investigated the universal provision in each of our five classes by auditing classroom provision using the school's adapted universal provision matrices alongside the document 'Devon Graduated Response Tool' (Devon County Council 2017). This specified a non-negotiable basic level of resources, systems and approaches to learning which were categorised within a universal provision map under the four areas of SEN need (cognition and learning; communication and interaction; physical and/or sensory; and social, emotional and mental health). These non-negotiables included:

- a visual timetable in every classroom using an arrow to show 'now' and 'next' labelled trays with words and pictures
- visual resources on every table to support English and Maths such as phonic sound mats and number lines; and visual prompt cards to support learning, for example, good listening/sitting
- clear, uncluttered workspaces.

This audit form was designed as a traffic light rating system (red = not evident; amber = emerging signs of progress; green = evident/working well) and asked teachers to indicate whether their classroom environment clearly shows that appropriate provision is in place. The audit was followed by a staff meeting to discuss our findings, improve our practice and plan our next steps.

As a result of this initial evaluative study, I analysed these data to highlight which resources were evident and which needed sourcing, and where staff training was needed. The findings from this analysis led to a follow up research study on the impact of our subsequent actions to increase our universal provision. Our headteacher used the matrices to inform all staff of non-negotiable resources that she would expect every classroom to have – these included a visual timetable, labelled trays, visual resources for English and Maths, use of social stories, visual prompts to support learning, clear marking policy – and that these would be audited by room each term. Where resources had to be sourced, I funded this from our SEN budget or made the resources. Where staff training was required, I liaised with the headteacher and we ensured that a staff meeting to support their professional development (CPD) was in place. I then provided the training as part of my role of SENDCO or sourced an outside agency to lead it for sessions that included:

- a staff meeting on Social Stories, to enable staff to use these to support children's social and emotional needs
- a Maths CPD staff meeting on Talk Expectations
- a staff meeting linked to my Devon Enhanced Autism Program (DEAP) training on 'Communication and interaction'
- a staff meeting on 'Speech, language and communication' where I used a presentation first delivered by an advisory teacher on my National Award Special Educational Needs course.

The original audit process was then repeated each term, using staff meetings to discuss our latest findings, continue to improve our practice and plan next steps.

Collecting evidence to measure impact

Evidence collection

Current methods of data collection within schools tend to include both qualitative and quantitative approaches. A wide range of techniques are used to collect qualitative data, including observations, interviews and focus groups, all of which can be used in a single school setting. Qualitative methods can involve parents, children and teachers answering questions, but this form of data collection can be perceived as subjective (Wolcott 1994). Quantitative data involves the gathering of numerical data that can be measured numerically and more precisely, so is less likely to be interpreted in different ways (Hohmann 2006), but it can be argued that such data fails to capture the realities of individual situations. Connelly (2007) maintains, however, that both types of data collection can be used very successfully, but for different purposes and Thomas (2017) identifies the importance of using a range of methods to provide complementary insights.

For my action research study, I adopted a mixed method research strategy that involved collecting both quantitative and qualitative data. Although this approach can take more time to plan and implement, I believe that adopting it provided a fuller picture of the universal provision that our school has in place, identifying the opinions of the teachers and the positive impact that enhancing universal provision is having on the children and their learning.

Prior to carrying out the initial audit of universal provision in each class, I sent every teacher a letter to explain clearly all about the study and thank them for their support in helping to ensure that the school was meeting its responsibilities under the new SEN Code of Practice. My subsequent action research was not mentioned in that letter, so I had to send out another letter informing the teachers about my further study and request their consent for this, ensuring that they understood the process and why their participation was necessary. Since this research exceeded normal teaching functions, the informed consent of participants was required. All teachers were advised that their names and that of the school would not be included in the research report and that all responses would be anonymised, thereby preserving confidentially in line with BERA (2018) ethical guidelines.

In addition to collecting the quantitative data through the universal matrices each term, I also sent out a questionnaire to collect the five teachers' opinions on the impact that raising the profile of universal provision within the school was having on the children's learning. This provided valuable qualitative data which was then supplemented by my classroom observations for triangulation purposes. These involved me taking on the role of a participant observer, which DeWalt and DeWalt (2002) suggest can be used to increase the validity of a study through helping researchers gain a better understanding of the context. The observations enabled me to confirm which resources were evident and which needed further development, and to engage in professional dialogue about strategies for ensuring that all classrooms are resourced to support SEN-designated children. This participant observer role allowed me to become involved in the activities that I was researching, spend time with participants to build relationships and adopt a more collaborative style of working; all of which I view as a key part of my role as SENDCO.

When I led a focused CPD session for the original evaluative audit, I first outlined the four areas of SEN provision and ensured that all staff had a shared understanding of each area and the resources listed within them. Then they evaluated their classroom resources using the traffic light rating system and were invited to identify any queries for further discussion. I explained that I would support them in addressing areas of weakness that were identified through the evaluative process. The traffic light system was adopted because it would provide an initial school-wide overview of compliance, identify any areas requiring immediate attention and permit comparative and trending analysis when repeated. Teachers were confident about using this system as it is used in other areas of school evaluation.

Impact

My findings capture an overview of the four areas of SEN provision in each class across the school, focusing on resources. The tables below

(Tables 9.1–9.6) compare the findings collated from the audits, identifying percentages for each area of provision and the resources which are evident in each class (the five classes are labelled C1, C2, C3, C4 and C5).

The information that was collected in the questionnaires identified teachers' knowledge about high quality universal provision and how confident they were with using a range of resources which would support all children – but especially those with SEN. They had been asked what different visual resources were being used that would cater for children in the four areas of SEN and whether tasks were being

Table 9.1 Cognition and learning

Traffic light system	% of resources in C1	% of resources in C2	% of resources in C3	% of resources in C4	% of resources in C5
Red	11%	6%	6%	11%	6%
Amber	22%	17%	22%	22%	17%
Green	67%	77%	72%	67%	77%

Table 9.2 Communication and interaction

Traffic light system	% of resources in C1	% of resources in C2	% of resources in C3	% of resources in C4	% of resources in C5
Red	23%	8%	4%	15%	15%
Amber	23%	15%	27%	23%	15%
Green	54%	77%	69%	62%	70%

Table 9.3 Physical and sensory

Traffic light system	% of resources in C1	% of resources in C2	% of resources in C3	% of resources in C4	% of resources in C5
Red	18%	0%	0%	0%	6%
Amber	12%	0%	0%	18%	12%
Green	70%	100%	100%	82%	82%

Table 9.4 Behaviour, emotional and social development

Traffic light system	% of resources in C1	% of resources in C2	% of resources in C3	% of resources in C4	% of resources in C5
Red	28%	0%	4%	12%	8%
Amber	12%	12%	24%	12%	16%
Green	60%	88%	72%	76%	76%

Table 9.5 Summary of findings

	Cognition and learning	Communication and interaction	Physical and sensory	BESD	Overall school performance measure
Red	10%	13%	5%	10%	10%
Amber	20%	21%	8%	15%	16%
Green	70%	66%	87%	75%	74%

Table 9.6 Comparison of the autumn and summer term data

	Cognition and learning		Communication and interaction		Physical and sensory		BESD		Overall school performance measure	
Red	31%	10%	33%	13%	24%	5%	24%	10%	28%	10%
Amber	24%	20%	21%	21%	12%	8%	17%	15%	19%	16%
Green	45%	70%	46%	66%	64%	87%	59%	75%	53%	74%

Summer term data is indicated in the table in italics.

Key: Green = area of provision where most resources are evident
      Red = area of provision where resources require attention

differentiated for children with SEN, with evidence of this in their books. They were also asked about a range of resources accessible for children and if they had the knowledge and understanding of how to use them independently to support their learning. The questionnaires went out to all of the teachers and I analysed their responses alongside my own observations that had focused on where and what universal provision was evident, and which areas we needed to make improvements.

When I first carried out my observations there was no evidence of visual resources to support the children; not all trays were labelled and there wasn't evidence of visual timetables being used in each class, or a consistent marking policy with differentiated work for children with SEN. After we had undertaken the audit, training and engaged in professional dialogue with staff members, there was clear evidence of the non-negotiables identified by the head teacher.

Since my research objective was to establish where improvements had taken place and the extent of these, my data analysis strategy also involved comparing key findings from the audit data with overall school performance data of provision. This provided me with an indication of our progress towards universal provision at whole-school level.

The findings highlighted areas of strength in provision and areas that still required improvement:

- C1 had the highest percentage of red ratings overall in the autumn and summer term audits. It was noted that this teacher was a NQT and although a programme of monitoring and support was subsequently put into place, the lack of experience and training required compared to the other teachers meant that this would remain an area to work on and support going forward.
- 'Communication and interaction' was identified in the autumn term audit as an area for development because it had the highest percentage of red rated resources. The summer term audit data suggested that this area still required development, although the percentage graded red had dropped from 33% to 13%. Overall, this was the second highest decrease, suggesting that the resources and collaboration put into place since the autumn term audit were having a positive effect and that significant progress was being made.
- The autumn term audit data revealed a significant gap between the resources evident in C1 and C2, especially in the areas of 'Communication and interaction' and 'Physical and sensory' provision. The summer term audit data continued to show a similar significant gap, although the percentage of green ratings increased in C1 from 42% to 70% in 'Communication and interaction' provision and from 41% to 54% in 'Physical and sensory'. This suggests that the modelling and promoting of effective practice, combined with collaborative working and regular careful monitoring, were improving the level of evident resources and their effective usage. However, these findings might also be partially attributable to the different cohorts in each class and the level of input from outside agencies to support the children in C2.

- In C3 the autumn term audit data revealed a high percentage of red ratings within 'Physical and sensory' provision, although there was also a high percentage of green within this class. The summer term audit data indicated that this was an area of great success since C3 now showed a green rated provision of 100% for 'Physical and sensory'. This resulted from staff CPD training, significant levels of input from outside agencies to support the high levels of SEN needs in that class and a practitioner who was willing to be flexible with, and reflect on, her own practice.
- Autumn term audit data suggested an adequate overall level of evident 'Physical and sensory' resources, with the highest overall school percentage evidenced in this area. Summer term audit data confirmed that this continued to be the highest performing area overall at 87%, compared to the lowest of 'Communication and interaction' at 66%.
- The overall school performance of universal provision figure increased from 53% shown as green rated in the autumn term audit to 74% in the summer term audit, indicating a significant improvement in the school's universal provision. This positive trend showed the impact of the CPD initiatives and classroom improvements at school level.

Next steps

Having gathered data at termly intervals and analysed my findings, I plan to continue monitoring the universal provision in each class to ensure that the teachers continue to reflect upon the resources in their own classrooms. Over the next school year I will also continue to work on the 'Communication and interaction' area of provision, providing opportunities for children to work across classes and key stages. I shall also be exploring the uses of interaction resources within this area, as well as maintaining discussions about provision in other schools with the SENDCOs from across our Academy to promote positive accessible routes of improvement already in our systems (Bartram 2015). I have already planned for a CPD staff meeting with an advisory teacher for dyslexia and booked specific members of staff onto some new training run by our county's Communication and Interaction Team looking at 'Enhanced Language'. I will also continue to use my role as SENDCO to support my colleagues, especially those who are NQTs and new to the profession, to share good practice and model the effective use of provision within my own classroom.

Recommendations

Recommendations for practice

This initial evaluative study was the start of a larger ongoing action research that involved a continuous cycle of assessing, planning, reviewing and doing. This cyclical, reflective and collaborative process enabled the careful monitoring of planned changes in practice.

The continuity between the two studies permitted me to assess our school's progress towards providing universal provision at different levels as outlined in the 2015 Code of Practice and the Element 3 Matrices (2013–2015). Using these matrices has enabled me to facilitate targeted initiatives, manage any CPD needs, improve the resources held in school and engage in professional dialogue with my colleagues. It was important to work collaboratively with colleagues to enable them to take ownership over their classroom provision, target specific areas of provision that require it and learn from the strengths of colleagues through the sharing of good practice.

As we are part of an Academy, this good practice will not be isolated within our own school but can be shared across all 12 schools. This provides us with the flexibility to observe and benefit from each other's practice and strengths. Overall, a school's performance measure provides a simple indicator of progress at school level, enabling a SENCO to monitor this and make comparisons with previous data. It will also allow SENCOs to quickly identify any changes that need to be addressed and roll out across the school.

When reflecting on my research practice, I am pleased that I made the decision to elect for a termly audit of universal provision instead of an annual one, which I did briefly consider when starting my study. I feel that by collecting data termly and analysing the results, I am able to gain a much better understanding of the areas and class of need, and can quickly initiate any changes. It also allows for continued dialogues between colleagues and provision to be monitored regularly to ensure that we are constantly striving to support all children in our classes.

I feel that this study has demonstrated how 'trend analysis' can be combined with diagnostic intervention-orientated research ('trend analysis' involves projections – calculating how a particular variable will be affected if a trend continues). Given the SENCO remit and workload, plotting the school performance figure over time (on a termly basis) enables SENCOs to supply governors, head teachers and Ofsted, with a headline figure that is an indicator of the school's performance in the area of universal provision. However, from the SENCO perspective, such monitoring also provides a point of comparison for diagnostic purposes and ensures that schools focus their attention and actions on areas that have the most impact on overall performance (Gavett 2016). Termly monitoring raises the profile of universal provision and ensures that it is a priority within each class.

Moving forwards, I feel that our matrices can be increased as we learn more about the needs of the children in our school and through our own professional development and learning. I will continue to monitor our universal provision termly, sharing the results with school staff and other Academy SENDCOs, and hope to see the percentages increasing in each area.

Recommendations for reading

Bartram, D. (2015) *Ten Steps to Effective SEN provision Special Educational Needs*. Available online at: www.senmagazine.co.uk/articles/articles/senarticles/ten-steps-to-effective-sen-provision (Accessed 19/12/18)

A clear guide to inform you of effective SEN provision needed in a classroom.

Department for Education (2015) *Special Educational Needs and Disability Code of Practice*, London: HMSO

The statutory Code of Practice for SEN to which all schools need to adhere.

Devon County Council (2017) *Devon Graduated Response Tool*, Devon: DCC & Babcock. Available online at: www.babcockldp.co.uk/disadvantaged-vulnerable-learners/send/devon-graduated-response (Accessed 19/12/18)

A tool kit to highlight universal, specific and targeted provision to support teachers and SEN pupils.

References

British Educational Research Association (2018) *Ethical Guidelines for Education Research*, London: BERA

Connelly, P. (2007) *Quantitative Data Analysis in Education*, London: Sage Publications

Department for Education (2015) *Special Educational Needs and Disability Code of Practice*, London: HMSO

Devon County Council (2017) *Devon Graduated Response Tool*Devon: DCC & Babcock. Available online at: www.babcockldp.co.uk/disadvantaged-vulnerable-learners/send/devon-graduated-response (Accessed 19/12/18)

DeWalt, K.M. and DeWalt, B.R. (2002) *Participant Observation: A Guide for Fieldworkers*, Walnut Creek, CA: AltaMira Press

Gavett, G. (2016) The Long-term Effects of Tracking Employee Behavior. Available online at: https://hbr.org/2016/07/the-long-term-effects-of-tracking-employee-behavior (Accessed 13/05/19)

Hohmann, U. (2006) *Quantitative Methods in Education Research*, Buckingham: Open University Press

Thomas, G. (2017) *How to Do Your Research Project: A Guide for Students*, London: Sage

Waters-Adams, S. (2006) *Education Action Research*. Available online at: www.tandfonline.com/doi/pdf/10.1080/09650790300200210?needAccess=true (Accessed 07/05/19)

Wolcott, H. (1994) *Transforming Qualitative Data*, London: Sage Publications

The impact of the *Special Educational Needs and Disabilities Code of Practice: 0–25 Years* on relationships between SENCOs, parents and colleagues

Katherine Smith

Context

The *Special Educational Needs and Disabilities Code of Practice: 0–25* (DfE and DoH 2015) was first published in 2014 and updated in 2015. It explains the duties of local authorities, health services, schools and colleges to provide for children with Special Educational Needs and Disabilities (SEND) under Part 3 of the Children and Families Act 2014. This document replaced the 2001 'Special Educational Needs (SEN): Code of Practice' and created perhaps the biggest shake up in the UK education system for children with SEND in the last 30 years. A key point in the new Code of Practice (CoP) of particular interest to me was 'a clearer focus on the views of children, young people and parents in the decision making at individual and strategic levels' (DfE and DoH 2015: 14). Involving parents in all aspects of decision making, including how the money provided by their local authority is spent on their child, represents a huge cultural shift from the previous code.

The role of the SENCO was first formalised and defined in the Special Educational Needs Code of Practice (DfE 1994) and reviewed in 1998 following the Government's list of Standards (TTA 1998). These professional competencies were retained in the Revised Special Educational Needs Code of Practice (DfE 2001). Subsequent developments have meant that the position of the SENCO role within school staffing structures has changed dramatically over the last twenty years and I believe it is still in a period of transition. Prior to 2009 when the Training and Development Agency for Schools (TDA) created nationally accredited training for SENCOs, there had been no recognised award for them: this is now a requirement for all new SENCOs. Further requirements now also state that a SENCO must be a qualified teacher, which has raised the status of this role in some schools. The House of Commons' Education and Skills Select Committee (2006) recommended that SENCOs should be a member of the senior leadership team, which I believe, indicates their perception of this role having a formal leadership status. However, this was not passed as a statutory requirement, so was not adopted by all schools.

My own personal experience as a SENCO and a mother of a child with disabilities has given me more experience than most SENCOs of what it is like to be working within the guidelines of the CoP and experiencing how it is impacting on my own child's provision. Families of children with SEND increasingly find they must battle to find help and feel concerned that their schools do not have the incentive to help their children. With budgets so tight, parents often demand explanations on how their personal budgets are being spent. The irony is that since the SEND Reforms, the focus should be more on the outcome for children and less on the provision which they receive. The desperate shortage of services for children with SEND in my area, I would argue, has left SENCOs struggling to make provision for the children they are trying to support and created significant challenges for the role. In addition, neo-liberalism and the impact of austerity programmes have forced schools and local authorities to put even greater strain on the relationship between parents and schools.

Since the 2015 CoP, the Department for Education (DfE) has conducted several surveys regarding how the new provision is shaping. In November 2017, the tenth DfE SEND survey illustrated that only 5% of children felt they were fully involved in the decisions made about their SEN provision and just 10% of parents felt they were fully involved. In 2009, Lamb envisioned that engaged parents would be more informed and actively involved with their child's education if a stake holder environment was created. I would argue, considering these very low statistics, Lamb's vision has yet to be realised (DCSF 2009). Skipp and Hopwood's report (2016) highlighted how parents were not satisfied with the Education, Health and Care Plan (EHCP) experience. The situations they found especially frustrating included: the provision of suitable support to meet their child's needs; ensuring plans were put into action and reviewed regularly; securing 'joined up' multi-agency working; and consideration of the child's own longer-term ambitions. I would argue that it is the SENCOs' role to achieve these goals through working with parents, although SENCOs are not mentioned explicitly within this report. Despite the 2015 CoP moving into its fourth year, current DfE surveys are not showing any significant improvement in parental satisfaction. If anything, this has plateaued, suggesting there is a complicated problem that warrants deeper investigation where the role of SENCO is fully considered.

Strategy

The aim of this study was to explore how the introduction of the 2015 CoP has impacted SENCOs' relationships with parents and colleagues. Insight gained into some of the challenges experienced would then be used to inform recommendations for practice.

A mainly qualitative research approach was adopted to collect evidence of SENCOs' experiences. The ideal study would have been to reach a very broad audience for my survey, drawing on SENCOs working in different boroughs and types of settings to test if results can be generalised. However, creating a large-scale survey would have been difficult to manage, given the short timescale available to me. The cohort I had most access to were fellow student SENCOs studying for their National SENCO Award. Having heeded the advice of research literature which suggested higher response rates were possible when the data collector has some relationship to the respondents, my student colleagues were a logical choice. This gave me a potential of twenty SENCO responses, which I felt that despite being a small sample size, was large enough to identify useful findings from the data collected.

The questionnaire I designed was influenced by three main sources:

- My unique experience as both a mother of a child with additional needs and a SENCO.
- An 'expert interview' – the interviewee was a semi-retired SENCO trainer with nearly 40 years of experience of working in education. This interview was held very early on in my cycle of research and influenced my choice of questions. Data collected from this interview helped me to focus on the struggles that were hindering positive relationships with parents – one of the main points being parents seemed to have an unrealistic view of what the role of SENCO entailed.
- Finally the literature review which highlighted that:
  a there was much written on the need for SENCOs to engage with parents (Hallett and Hallett 2017; Wearmouth 2016; Hornby 2011) but little literature on the practicalities of 'how' to do this

b   the role of the SENCO varied enormously from setting to setting (Tissot 2013) and although it is recommended in the new CoP that SENCOs are part of the Senior Management team, this isn't always the case

c   if parents feel as if they have to 'fight' to get the support they want for their children (Nettleton and Friel 2015), the SENCO can often bear the brunt of those parents' frustrations (Wolfendale 2017).

This led me to pose an additional question: What training have SENCOs received on working with parents, conflict resolution or mediation?

Collecting evidence to measure impact

Evidence collection

Twenty SENCOs were surveyed via emailed questionnaires using SurveyMonkey (I will refer to this group as S20). I asked ten questions which focused on: 1) how SENCOs fitted into their school's leadership team; 2) how realistic were parents and colleagues' expectations of them; 3) whether there had there been more or less conflict between themselves and parents since the new CoP, and the causes of any conflict; and 4) any useful training they had received on how to work with parents.

To triangulate the survey data, I then interviewed two SENCOs – one very experienced senior manager and another who was new to the role – to discover their perceptions and experiences of working as a SENCO. The more experienced SENCO (SENCO 1) was able to talk at length about the role, making particular reference to his experience of conflicts between SENCOs and parents. He was able to draw on his experiences before and after the 2015 CoP. My second interviewee was the SENCO new to the role (SENCO 2). She only had a year's experience of the role so was not asked to reflect on the new CoP changes. I considered the vulnerability of this new SENCO, especially as I was asking interviewees to reveal things about themselves they would not typically share with others. I also explained to the S20 group that I was looking to support SENCOs, not discredit them in anyway. I explained how the data (i.e. the interview transcripts and surveys) would be securely stored and responses anonymised. The interviews were conducted in a neutral environment of the interviewees choosing.

Impact

Three themes emerged from my collected data.

Theme 1: How SENCOs fit into the senior leadership team

The new CoP notes that because SENCOs have a crucial role to play in determining the strategic development of SEND policy and provision for children with SEND within schools, they are more effective if they are part of the school senior leadership team. Thirteen of S20 were part of the senior leadership team, including one head teacher and one deputy. All 13 senior leaders worked in school full time, although their SENCO responsibilities were coupled with a part-time teaching post. Most of this group commented on this enhancing their ability to "raise the profile of the SENCO within the school" and found "being accessible to parents throughout the week a real positive".

Seven of S20 indicated that their colleagues had unrealistic expectations of them as SENCOs. Ekins (2015) argued that there was previously an over-identification of children who were underachieving as having SEN, with the 'knock on' effect that some teachers shifted responsibility for the learning of children with SEN away from themselves onto their SENCO. The CoP has forced a shake-up in relationships between SENCOs and class teachers. It states that teachers are responsible and accountable for the progress and development of all the pupils in their class, including those on the school SEND register (DfE and DoH 2015). I would argue that although there is now an understanding that teachers are ultimately responsible for every child's education, this accountability brings additional pressures for class teachers. As a result, in some situations, the historic SENCO role – where children with additional needs were categorised neatly and passed to the SENCO – must be a difficult attitude to shake. This reflects Shields' argument (2013) that when educators are forced to change, they often fall back onto past behaviours, describing these as "best practice" and so in this situation, contribute to unrealistic expectations of SENCOs.

Theme 2: The success of SENCOs' working partnerships with parents

Nine respondents thought that parents' expectations of them were unrealistic. All who made comments on this referred to expectations parents had about time management, for example: "Requesting meetings regularly, expect results instantly!" and "Unrealistic, because I am only one person and I cannot always do what they would like me to do given the number of children on my work load." Ten of the S20 viewed parents' expectations of them as realistic. Generally, this group had more than three years of experience of being a SENCO so it could be that they were generally more positive people who were better at accommodating change themselves, or it could be that they had more years of working since the 2015 CoP, so were more able to embrace the changes that it bought. Perhaps, as Cheminais (2013) writes, they embraced 'skills of resilience' and have been able to cope with setbacks.

SENCO 1 felt that parents' views of the SENCO role were unrealistic "mainly because they are ignorant of what the position involves". He remarked on his experience of working in different primary schools: "In previous schools I've worked in, the SENCO sits in an office and can be quite anonymous to parents; it's not until the child needs a 'SENCO' that parents find out that the role exists at all." This suggests that the SENCO's role is not well advertised in all schools and Harris' view (Harris et al. 2009) – that creating positive relationships with parents benefit children's learning, but this must be at the centre of all aspects of school life and not 'bolt on' – has yet to be realised.

When asked to reflect on how easy she found it to engage with parents, SENCO 2 said:

> I find some parents really hard to deal with; some have unhappy memories of schools and being back in a school office make them want to rebel all over again! I think sometimes they like to try and get the upper hand. It's like they have an issue with me before we even start.

This reflects Baumgartner's theory (2001) that parents may feel subordinate to the team around the child and the SENCO can be seen as an authoritative figure. It would also suggest that Mezirow's ideal (Mezirow et al. 2009) of a learning environment where all participants are viewed as equal, is possibly difficult to achieve in some schools – an issue identified for further development by the EEF (2018) and Education Scotland (2019).

SENCOs were asked if there had been more conflict with parents since the new CoP or if relationships with parents had strengthened and improved. Five respondents stated that there had been more conflict, six thought there had been less and nine others reported no change. When asked to state what caused conflict between themselves and parents, all SENCOs made reference to not being able to offer the desired level of support from outside agencies, with one explaining:

> Our local authority has not been able to fill the Educational Psychologist vacancies so we've not been able to get an Ed Psych into our school this term.

This quote highlights a typical gap between what parents expect from SENCOs and what they are able to provide. It also reflects the National Education Union's claim (2019) that special needs provision in England has lost out on '£1.2bn because of shortfalls in funding increased from central government since 2015'. Local authority budgets are being stretched to the brink; in part due to the extension of education health care planned provision to include young people with additional needs aged 19–25, without extending funding.

All six of the S20 that made positive comments about the new CoP's impact on their relationships with parents described how parents were encouraged to come into school more often. SENCO 1 elaborated on the benefits he had seen since the latest CoP:

> We [our school] definitely encourage parents to come into school more. Not just children with SEND, but all parents. There seem to be more parents' evenings, coffee mornings and opportunities for teachers to work with parents.

I asked why this was happening and he replied: "We have had a new headteacher recently, he seems a bit more on the ball and he seems to be moving things forward better. I think my last headteacher just saw parents as a bit of a nuisance!" This relates to Hornby's view (2011) that the 'professional distance' some teachers have adopted in the past has not progressed parent–teacher relations, possibly because of the lack of training they have received on how to work with parents and so this is an ongoing challenge for schools (Education Scotland 2019).

Theme 3: SENCOs have been thrust into the role of mediator, negotiator or conflict resolver and agents for change, but may not feel equipped for the job

None of the SENCOs surveyed had received any useful training on how to engage with parents or manage confrontation. When I asked SENCO 1 if he had been asked to intervene in parental conflict, he reported:

> I am called to support the NQTs all the time. I think some of them could do with a few pointers of how to communicate with parents better. They can be very defensive. Sometimes parents want to see

more senior staff and I get that, but often it's because the teachers feel a bit out of their depth.

SENCO 2 had not had any training on mediation or conflict resolution, or in fact any training on how to engage with parents. I asked her if she thought this would be useful, she replied:

> Oh my, yes, totally. I used to work in retail a long time ago. I had training in dealing with conflict resolution then. I use some of those techniques now you know. I don't remember receiving any offer of courses while I was studying (PGCE). I might have when I was an NQT, but I don't think so.

Conclusions

My research findings suggest that the 2015 CoP has not acknowledged SENCOs are the lynchpin that holds the team around the child together and 'coordinates' support for families. SENCOs are hugely influential in the parental experience. With funding now being given directly to schools in order to make provision for children with SEND, schools have an increased responsibility to be accountable for how this money is being spent. This has created tension, placing the SENCO in a mediatory role between parents, colleagues, health professionals and their local authority – a role in which relationships are key. The DfE (2018) highlights that 14.6% of children in England have special educational needs. I would argue SENCOs have a much better chance of being effective in their role if they are part of the senior leadership team and are able to adopt a strategic approach to leading SEND within their school.

The Code of Practice (2015) asks SENCOs to embrace a new ethos and ways of working, but says nothing on 'how' to involve parents in decision making. SENCOs have been manoeuvred into the role of agents for change, but do they feel equipped for the job? What do *they* feel have been the barriers to achieving their CoP goals? Have SENCOs found their own way to do this and are they demonstrating 'best practice' or falling back into previous ways of working? These are the questions I feel that have yet to be asked, but are critical to improving the parental experience. I believe the CoP needs to move away from a focus on 'need' towards the 'human rights' of children and their families (Sayers 2018). This all leads me to suggest that there is a need for more research on how SENCOs have adapted to this role and how they can improve the parental experience.

Recommendations

Recommendations for practice

In my experience, the most effective way of raising your profile within the school is simply to outline to parents and staff what the role of the SENCO involves. Since the new CoP, I would stress the importance of having an School Information Report that is clear and meaningful for parents. There are many opportunities for SENCOs to speak to parents over the course of the academic year. I often found 'new parents" information evenings provided a great opportunity to introduce myself. I would prepare a short presentation at these sessions, always assuming that parents knew very little about my role and how it fitted within the senior leadership team. I think it is important at these presentations to outline how you can help link them to health, education and social care, and how the children and their families will be able to shape the support that is available to them. Using the School Information Report as a basis for your presentation is a really effective way of sharing this information.

There is a gap in the literature with regard to SENCOs finding support on how to be negotiators, conflict resolvers and mediators. My research highlighted that newly qualified teachers may not be receiving any specific training on how to engage with parents and only one of the 20 SENCOs surveyed had any useful training on conflict resolution or mediation. In the long term, I would argue, mediation should be a compulsory part of teacher training and the National Award for SEN Co-ordination.

I believe mediation begins with first establishing lines of communication. I find being consistent and reliable in terms of being contactable helps to build trust with parents and helps relationships to grow; the logistics of this communication needs careful consideration if the SENCO is not a full-time member of staff. As a SENCO I always try to furnish parents with the means to communicate with me on a regular basis and keep open the channels of communication, whether this is via email, face-to-face, or over the telephone. As my research suggested, conflicts can arise when colleagues do not have realistic expectations of SENCOs. I feel it is important to consider that even longer-serving teachers may be uncertain of the role of the SENCO since the new Code of Practice; taking the lead at a staff meeting to set out your responsibilities and how you can support them with theirs can help inform teachers.

It will be difficult to regulate how parents are perceived and welcomed into partnerships within schools. I would suggest that the ethos of parental involvement depends very much on the attitudes of headteachers and senior leadership teams. The literature evidence on how parental involvement increases children's attainment has long been acknowledged (Harris et al. 2009; Epstein and Sheldon 2002; Fan and Chen 2001) – and more recently by the EEF (2018) and Education Scotland (2019). More creative and immediate ways of involving parents in their children's learning need to be considered – for example, using class blogs, messenger apps such as ParentMail, regularly updated websites, Twitter feeds and secure assessment sharing online could be a fluid way of communicating with parents. This should mark a move away from the rigidity of structured invitations into school for parent evenings and end of year report writing. In terms of policy recommendations, I think that this all needs to be considered in revised versions of the CoP, identifying exactly 'how' to involve parents and how to resolve associated gaps in training for SENCOs and teachers.

Recommendations for reading

Freeman, G. (2016) *SEN and Parental Engagement*. Available online at: www.sec-ed.co.uk/best-practice/sen-and-parental-engagement (Accessed 13/03/19)

This article summarises many great research guides to parental involvement and links it back to the Lamb report. It offers practical advice to parents and teachers.

Runswick Cole, K., Curran, T. & Liddiard, K. (eds.) (2018) *The Palgrave Handbook of Disabled Children's Childhood Studies*, London: Palgrave Macmillan

This handbook provides a global account of children with special educational needs and brings together many different perspectives from parents, children, academics and activists.

Done, L., Murphy, M. and Watt, A. (2017) *Change Management and the SENCo Role: Developing Key Performance Indicators in Strategic Development of Inclusivity*. Available online at: https://onlinelibrary. wiley.com/doi/full/10.1111/1467-9604.12138 (Accessed 02/02/19)

This article highlights the changing role of SENCOs in England and how they are required to manage change strategically and deliver inclusive school cultures.

References

Baumgartner, L. (2001) An Update on Transformative Learning, *New Directions for Adults in Continuing Education*, 89: 15–24

Cheminais, R. (2013) *Promoting and Developing School-to-School Support for Special Educational Needs*, Abingdon: Routledge

Department for Education (DfE) (1994) *The Code of Practice for the Identification of Special Educational Needs Code of Practice*, London: DfE

Department for Education and Skills (DfES) (2001) *Special Educational Needs Code of Practice*, London: DfES

Department for Education (DfE) (2017) *Tenth Special Educational Needs and Disability (SEND) Reforms Implementation Survey For Parent Carer Forums Autumn 2017*. Available online at: contact.org.uk (Accessed 09/01/19)

Department for Education (DfE) (2018) *Special Educational Needs in England – January 2018: main text*. Available online at: www.gov.uk (Accessed 25/04/19)

Department for Education and Department for Health (DfE and DoH) (2015) *Special Educational Needs and Disabilities Code of Practice: 0–25 Years*, London: DfE & DoH

Department for Children, Schools and Families (DCSF) (2009) *Lamb Inquiry: Special Educational Needs and Parental Confidence*, Nottingham: DCSF

Education Scotland (2019) *Engaging Parents and Families. Involving All Parents*, Livingstone: Education Scotland

Education Endowment Foundation (EEF) (2018) *Working With Parents to Support Children's Larning. Guidance Report*, London: EEF

Ekins, A. (2015) *The Changing Face of Educational Needs: Impact and Implications for SENCOs, Teachers and their Schools*, Abingdon: Routledge

Epstein, J.L. and Sheldon, S.B. (2006) Present and Accounted for: Improving student attendance through family and community involvement, *The Journal of Education Research*, 95: 308–318

Fan, X.T. and Chen, M. (2001) Parental involvement and students' academic achievement: A meta-analysis, *Educational Psychology Review*, 13: 1–22

Hallett, F. and Hallett, G. (2017) *Transforming the Role of the SENCO*, Maidenhead: McGrawHill/Open University Press

Harris, A., Andrew-Power, K. and Goodall, J. (2009) *Do Parents Know They Matter? Raising Achievement Through Parental Engagement*, London: Network Continuum Education

Harris, N. and Riddell, S. (2016) *Resolving Disputes about Educational Provision: A Comparative Perspective on Special Educational Needs*, Abingdon: Routledge

Hornby, G. (2011) *Parental Involvement in Childhood Education: Building Effective School – Family Partnerships*, London: Springer

House of Commons Select Committee on Education and Skills (2006) Third Report, 321–322. Available online at: www.parliament.uk (Accessed 16/08/19)

Mezirow, J., Taylor, E. and Associates (2009) *Transformative Learning in Practice: Insights from Community, Workplace and Higher Education*, San Francisco: Jossey-Bass

National Education Union (2019) *SEND Provision*. Available online at: neu.org.uk (Accessed 25/04/19)

Nettleton, M. and Friel, J. (2015) *Special Needs and Legal Entitlement: The Essential Guide to Getting out of the Maze*, London: Jessica Kingsley Publishers

Sayers, D. (2018) Rights not needs: Changing the legal model for Special Educational Needs (SEN). In Runswick-Cole, K., Curran, T. and Liddiard, K. (eds.) *The Palgrave Handbook of Disabled Children's Childhood Studies*, Basingstoke: Palgrave Ltd

Shields, R. (2013) *Globalisation and International Education*, London: Bloomsbury

Skipp, A. and Hopwood, V. (2016) *Mapping User Experiences of the Education, Health and Care Process: A qualitative study*. Available online at: https://assets.publishing.service.gov.uk/government/uploads/system/uploads/attachment_data/file/518963 (Accessed 23/03/2019)

Teacher Training Agency (TTA) (1998) *National Standards for Special Educational Needs Co-ordinators*, London: TTA

Tissot, C. (2013) The role of the SENCo as leaders, *British Journal of Sociology of Education*, 40: 33–40

Wearmouth, J. (2016) *The Effective SENCO; Meeting the Challenge*, Maidenhead: McGrawHill/Open University Press

Wolfendale, S. (2017) *Meeting Special Needs in the Early Years: Directions in Policy and Practice*, London: Taylor & Francis Group

Index

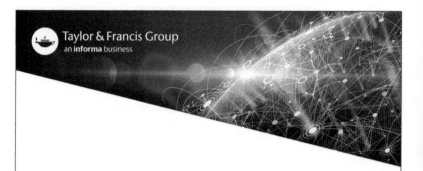